We are given situations and problems in this life so that our own spirit can also learn and grow. Without these lessons we are stagnant—we stop advancing, stop learning. The fact of the matter is, the more our souls gain from all of life's experiences, the closer we become to God.

It is up to us how close to God we want to be.

Photograph by Gayle Garnett

About Patrick Mathews

When, as a child, Patrick Mathews began seeing dead relatives appear, he had no idea this would lead to his life's work. Through his gift of mediumship, his demonstrations and readings have helped many people connect with loved ones who have passed over to the other side. He has appeared on numerous national television and radio shows, such as *The Rob Nelson Show, Leeza, Ryan Seacrest & Lisa Foxx Show*, WGN's *Steve Cochran Show, Jill and Friends*, as well as being featured on *ABC News*, and on PBS. Patrick has also produced a series of meditation CDs to help others make a connection to the other side.

Never Say GOODBYE

A Medium's Stories of Connecting With Your Loved Ones

PATRICK MATHEWS

2003
Llewellyn Publications
St. Paul, Minnesota, 55164-0383, U.S.A.

FIRST EDITION
First Printing, 2003

Book interior design and editing by Connie Hill
Cover design by Gavin Dayton Duffy
Cover image © 2002 by Photodisc

Library of Congress Cataloging-in-Publication Data
To come

Llewellyn Publications
A Division of Llewellyn Worldwide, Ltd.
P.O. Box 64383, Dept. 0-7387-0353-2
St. Paul, MN 55164-0383, U.S.A.
www.llewellyn.com

Printed in the United States of America

Dedication

This book is dedicated to my sister and best friend,
Kathy Mathews
... my **first** gift from God.

❧

Contents

Part VII: Last Words

Acknowledgments

First and foremost, I want to thank God and my Spirit Guide, Andrew. Without all of your love, help, and guidance . . . none of what I do would be possible.

To my wonderful and dear parents, James and Florence Mathews. From the day I was born, you taught me by example to always follow my dreams, help others in need, and to know the most important gift we can give, and receive, is love.

To everyone in my family who has offered their interest, love and support with this healing work I do. Thank you.

Uncle Edward . . . see what you started!

Jennie and Velma, your encouragement of my work has truly meant so much to me.

Jeff "Eff" Roth . . . I know, I know . . . you're welcome!

Gina "GG" Flowers, a great friend who really knows how to handle a crowd.

Carolyn "Seesta" Lollar, your smiling face and caring heart are always a gift.

Lisa Foxx, your friendship and kind soul are greatly valued.

Though it is impossible to mention everyone who has given me support with my work, I would like to acknowledge a few special souls: Linda Kelp, Mark Bolt, Sally Owens, May-Lily Lee, Ryan Seacrest, Jude Martin, Mary Lester, Jill Lawrence, Patte Purcell, Barbara Wagaman, Karen Foster, Leeza Gibbons, Sarah Duffin, Ann Oppenheim, Cammy Farone, Kathleen Marusak, Ann Kerns . . . your wonderful enthusiasm has been much appreciated!

To all who have given me a public platform in order to help others. Thank you!

A special nod to a few of my friends in spirit: Sharon, Andy, Jimmy, Two Feathers, Rusty, Ashley, Church . . . how happy and blessed I am to know you.

Thanks to my literary agent Al Zuckerman, Fay Greenfield, and everyone at Writers House. Your faith in this book has made it possible for love from the other side to reach many here.

Nancy Mostad, Lisa Braun, Connie Hill, Gavin Duffy, Jerry Rogers, Amy Martin, and everyone at Llewellyn. Your enthusiasm for this book can only be matched by the kindness of your hearts.

My most heartfelt gratitude to everyone whose stories are shared in this book. Your experiences will help many understand that love and relationships with those on the other side continue always.

And thank you everyone to whom I have given a reading. It has been a privilege meeting you and your loved ones in spirit.

Introduction

"Your husband, Fred, is saying that he wants to clear up something that you've read."

Linda sat silent.

"He is telling me you were reading a book that stated that by you continuing to talk with him, you are keeping him with you, and not allowing him to move on."

Linda broke down and started to cry.

"Yes," she said. "I read that our loved ones will stay around with us just for a little while, and then want to move on."

"'Linda,' he is telling me to ask you, 'Where would he want to go?!' You were his life here, and you will continue to be there. He's not going anywhere! He doesn't care what those books are telling you!"

Linda continued to cry, but now with relief and happiness.

Fred wanted me to give her the next statement loud and clear.

Fred said, "Linda, understand this . . . you are part of my Heaven."

As a medium, and throughout the many connections I have made for people, the one thing I find amazing is how many people believe in an afterlife, yet who also believe their passed loved ones have discontinued their connection with them. People are so accustomed to having a physical link to another that once they lose it after a passing, they feel, or are told, that they must "let go" of the emotions and connection they feel toward someone else. They feel they have to tell them "Goodbye."

I'm here to tell you this is not true.

A soul does continue to live after a passing, and, in fact, goes to Heaven. But is Heaven some far-away, distant place?

No, it is not.

With this book, you will discover there is no such thing as having to *let someone go*, or that you are keeping a spirit from *moving on*. Your loved ones in spirit have, and will always *continue* to be, a part of your life, and you never have to tell them goodbye.

Part I

❧

Discovering the gift

Growing up, I didn't have any idea that I was going to become a medium, though the signs were there. As you read on, you will discover, just as I did, events happened in my life that led me to where I am today.

1

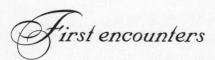

First encounters

While growing up, I had no idea, even in my wildest dreams, that I would become a medium . . . no idea at all.

So how and when did I discover I had the gift of communicating with Spirit?

The best way I can explain is to refer to the Kevin Costner film, *Field of Dreams*, one of my favorites.

In the film, Costner plays a farmer named Ray Kinsella. One day while plowing in his cornfield, Ray hears a voice coming from out of nowhere. Thinking the voice is simply a figment of his imagination, he continues working. No sooner does he start again than the voice comes back, louder and clearer this time, and he hears, "If you build it, he will come." At that moment, Ray sees a vision of a baseball diamond in his cornfield. Upon hearing this message and seeing this image of a baseball field, he feels a deep urge to plow up his cornfield to make the vision a reality. You don't have to be a farmer to know that this guy is nuts! But Ray goes along with his gut feeling, and down comes the corn, up goes the baseball field. Building the field did not answer his question about why he felt compelled to do this. In fact, this actually led to more visions and questions.

Throughout the movie, Ray travels on what seems to be a senseless journey, while following his visions and hunches. It is not until the end of the film we see that all his visions essentially *connect* with one another, forming a *whole picture*.

Why am I bringing this film up? No, I never wanted to build a baseball field, nor be a corn farmer. But events happened in my life that didn't make a lot of sense to me, either—that is, until I was able to see the whole picture. It was at that point I knew, and really came to understand, that my purpose in life would be to help people by connecting them with their loved ones who are on the other side.

Uncle Edward

One of my first face-to-face encounters with a spirit was with my Uncle Edward, who passed when I was about six years old. He was my mother's brother (one of many) who lived on an old plantation farm in Virginia, along with his siblings. Not long after his passing I was awakened one night by a noise. There in front of me I saw a figure standing next to my window. The image was that of a human, yet it, at first, had no distinct features. The first thought I had was that I must be dreaming, so I started to pinch my arm. I had heard if you were having a bad dream, by pinching yourself, you would awaken from it. *I didn't.* In fact, the more I pinched myself, the more it hurt. At that point, I knew I was fully awake and actually seeing what was in front of me. That led to only one other conclusion about what was happening. I said to myself, "Oh my God, it's a ghost!" Now, the smart thing for me to do would have been to run and get some help. I was too afraid, so I chose the second best thing—yes, to hide under the covers! When you're a kid, it always seems the safest place to be. After what I thought was plenty of time for the ghost to leave, I decided to peek out from under my blanket. What I saw was not a ghost, but my Uncle Edward standing there. He was not a solid person, nor transparent like the ghosts I had seen in cartoons. The best way I can describe him would be as a combination of both. Even though I was frightened, I could see that his face had a kind expression and it helped to calmed me down a bit. I remember thinking to myself: okay, he really is here, and I am actually seeing him. It was a mature reaction for a small boy, but what choice did I have? It seemed that I was going to face this ghost alone! What could or should I do next? I just kept looking at him standing next to my hoppity hop, and it seemed he was not going anywhere. While watching him, a thought came to me. More than a thought, it was a message—a message from Edward. He was letting me know that he was fine and still around, watching over the family. I also recall how much love I felt coming from him while receiving this message from him.

I thought, why me? Why was I seeing him? Was he going to show himself to anyone else?

I pulled those old safety blankets over me once more. This was a lot for me to take in, especially in the middle of the night and all alone. I started thinking to him, please leave, please leave. The next time I looked out, he was gone. Now was my chance to escape! I ran to my parents' bedroom and awakened my mother. I told her that I had just seen Edward, and he said he was still watching over us. The best part of all is that she never doubted me. She lovingly listened to all I had to say, and accepted my story of this visitation. And why not? Coming from a background of belief in an afterlife, it wasn't all that hard to conceive that our loved ones were around and watching over us.

I continued to see Uncle Edward every now and then, each time smiling at me, as if he had a secret.

Thinking back on that time, I had no idea that this was only the beginning.

Growing Up

My parents "Snooky" and Florence had six children, five boys and one girl. Kathy and I were the youngest of the bunch. As children, we two were always the closest and still are today. I feel very fortunate to have been raised in a small town in Virginia. Its beauty can only be matched by its rich and deep-rooted history.

Thinking back to my childhood, it seems I was always fascinated with ghosts. I remember the first Colorform set I ever owned was a haunted house. The kit consisted of little scary owls, ghosts, tombstones, and even a full moon, which I could stick all around the haunted house to make a scene. I played with that toy for hours on end.

Also remember "Kooky Spookys"? They were plastic, glow-in-the-dark, ghost finger puppets. I would hold them under a light for a few minutes and run into the closet. The eerie green glow would illuminate the dark room as I gave puppet shows for my family and friends. I loved those things!

On Saturday morning, my favorite cartoon was Scooby Doo. I enjoyed the characters' hunts for ghosts and goblins, and always pretended that I too was part of their gang.

One of my favorite films was *The Ghost and Mister Chicken*, starring Don Knotts. In the film, Don was dared to stay all night in a nearby haunted house. Didn't we all have one of those in our own neighborhood?

Just a block down from where I lived was an old house that had been abandoned for many years. Its paint, what was left of it, was peeling, and its shutters were falling off as well. The large steps leading to the front door had nail holes covered with rust, which we were told were bloody bullet holes from gangsters who had been shot on those very spots!

I would always walk by this house while going to the store or venturing off to play ball, but never had the courage to go in it. One day, on a dare by my friends, I got up enough nerve to go inside. I was about eight years old at the time, and knew I couldn't show how afraid I actually was. Climbing hesitantly through one of the windows on the side of the house, my buddies decided to assist by pushing me all the way in. The front door would most likely have been open, but how much more sneaky it was going in through a window. There was a strange smell to the house, reminiscent of old paint and must. As I walked around on the creaky floor, pushing the cobwebs away from my face, I started *sensing a presence there.* It was the type of feeling as if someone was watching me, and it made the hairs stand up on the back of my neck. While continuing to look around, very quickly I may add, I heard a noise coming from the upstairs portion of the house. *Klunk, klunk, klunk.* That was enough for me! I was not about to stick around and find out *who* or *what* it was. I jumped back out of the window, and told my friends who were waiting with anticipation, "Nope . . . . no ghosts in there!"

When you're eight years old, you have to be cool.

Ghost Taping

I also did the normal "scary" things that all kids do: telling ghost tales by candlelight and playing with a Ouija board. These were all different ways to try to scare one another.

I had once heard you could actually record the voice of a ghost. All you had to do was turn a tape recorder on, set the volume to the highest level, and leave it recording in an unoccupied room. The process seemed simple enough and sounded like fun. Of course, I didn't want to do this by myself, so I convinced my friend Vince to try it with me.

First, we had to find a tape recorder. We searched high and low at my house, to no avail, but we were not going to let these voices of the undead get away from us. We scoured Vince's basement until, in the corner, we found our key to the other side. We hurriedly grabbed the tape recorder and made sure that it worked—and of course it didn't. After going through drawer after drawer in search of fresh batteries, we finally got the recorder going.

Now, whose house were we going to use to let the "spirits" come through in? Vince said that, since it was his tape recorder, it should be his. I agreed. Also, there was no one else home at the time, and that was the way ghosts were supposed to like it. We set up the tape recorder, turned the volume as high as it would go, and left the room. We knew we couldn't stay alongside the recorder, as we would be making each other laugh too much and no ghost would ever come.

After about twenty minutes, we ran back into the room. We turned the recorder off, rewound the tape, pushed the play button, and waited to hear the messages from the other side. We listened very intently, but it seemed all we were hearing was static and we started laughing. After all this preparation we knew this had to work, so we listened longer—more static and more laughing. Then it happened! We both heard a voice. "Rewind, quick, rewind!" I shouted. We rewound the tape and there it was again, but what was the voice saying? There certainly was something on the tape; we just couldn't make it out. We almost wore that tape out rewinding it back and forth, until finally the message became clear, and it was only two words: "Spearmint gum!"

Correct, that was the message from a spirit from beyond the grave: Spearmint gum. We both heard it clear as a bell. We didn't have a clue what it meant, but we heard it, and had it on tape. We started laughing again, decided that we'd been successful, and celebrated with a Coke.

Later, Kathy and I attempted the same tape experiment with our friend Gina. She said she'd seen a ghost in her house many times, so why not try to record it? Being an old hand at this, and the man of the group, I set up the tape recorder and the rules. No one was to come into the room for at least a half hour. We all had to be together so we could be sure that no one could have tampered with the tape. Finally all was agreed upon and we started recording.

Once finished, as before, we listened for what seemed an eternity, but in actuality was about twenty minutes. We heard nothing but static, static, static. Then, out of nowhere, we heard a voice, a whispery haunting voice. It was soft and wavy, that of a woman. We played it several times and became more excited each time we heard it. The voice said, "Help me." Let me tell you, that was certainly different from "Spearmint gum"! We played it over again and all heard the same thing. Was this spirit really in need of help or was she just playing a trick on us? Who knows?

Medium Experience

Years later, Kathy and I were watching a daytime talk show that had a medium on as a guest. She told audience members about their loved ones who had passed, and we were amazed to see how accurate she was. We also wondered how it was possible for someone to have such an ability. We thought perhaps she had planted people in the audience, and this was some type of trick. Kathy decided to make an appointment with her, to see if she was for real. Success came in obtaining a phone session, and finally the day of the reading arrived. We were both excited to see if she would be able to communicate with any of our loved ones. Keep in mind that, with all the aunts and uncles we had on the other side, there should have been plenty of people eager to talk.

The medium started by telling us about our grandmother Mary. She described how Mary looked and how she had been watching over us. We had not known Mary, because she had passed before we were born, but Kathy had always sensed that she was around her.

The medium also talked about how close Kathy and I were, saying that we were as close as twins and that people sometimes mistook us for such (not physically, however, as I am six-foot-seven and Kathy is five-foot-seven). She also stated that Kathy was looking for a new car, and that she would find one that coming weekend. This was all true enough, as Kathy was looking for a car, and did in fact buy one that weekend. The medium went on and told us different facts about other people in our family. She also mentioned that we both had a *gift*, and would use it to help people. That was nice to hear, but we were more interested in what we could confirm about our loved ones on the other side.

So the reading was a success, and we realized that certain people do have this type of gift.

2

Gut feelings

California or Bust. Kathy and I decided to move to California, along with our good friend Jeff. For some reason, we were always being *pulled* to go there, and decided to give it a try. We both were interested in Hollywood, and thought it would be great to see what the place had to offer. The hardest part was leaving home. All of our family was in Virginia, and moving to the other side of the country would be difficult. But again, there was that gut instinct telling us we should go. We knew that we would come home on a regular basis, and call nightly to check up on the family. And if things didn't work out, we'd just pack up and head back! Kathy and I are kind of free-spirited when it comes to change.

So there we were, in Hollywood, California. Now what?

In time, I decided to take up film editing, and Kathy continued with her artwork. (She is a wonderful portrait artist.) Getting a job in the entertainment field is not easy, but with perseverance, I did it!

I was extremely excited as I drove to work that first day of my new Hollywood career, thinking about all the possibilities ahead. Behind the wheel, I said to myself, "Patrick, you are now succeeding in what you're supposed to be doing."

Then, something strange happened.

I heard another voice and it said, "This might be nice for now, but it's not what you are going to be doing."

I thought to myself, "Hey wait, where did that come from? I'm in Hollywood, I have a show biz career just starting, I'm going to meet celebrities and make some good money. Why isn't this what I'm going to be doing? It's what I want!"

The voice came back, "You'll see."

Ignoring the voice, I went on and launched my career as an editor.

Kathy had landed a job in a casting agency, but *she, too,* had a nagging feeling that something was just not right.

Opening Doors

In California, we had a chance to go to a demonstration by medium James Van Praagh. We had seen James on a television show called *The Other Side* and thought we would enjoy seeing him in person. James was not as well known then, but still he had a significant following. That night we witnessed remarkable things. James came out, answered questions, and gave random readings to members of the audience. Though we did not receive one, it was wonderful to see the healing effect that he was having on others.

After the demonstration, I started thinking about all the things I had seen that evening. I remembered one part of the lecture, in which James mentioned that though he had a gift, he had had to awaken it. At that moment, the *same* voice I had heard before in my head came to me and said, "You have the gift, too."

"Sure, right, I have a curiosity about this, but that's about it," I said to myself.

Yet there was a nagging sensation that I couldn't resist, urging me to find out more. So I did.

I started reading books about communicating with the other side. I found myself having to go to the "New Age" section of the bookstore before I could find any material on this subject. Believe me, in the past that was one section I never frequented. I had no interest in sitting under homemade pyramids, burning incense, or even wearing crystals. Not that there is anything wrong with any of the above—it just was not for me.

I worked myself through book after book, reading anything and everything on spirit communication. The more I read and learned about connecting with the other side, the stronger that *gut instinct* and *voice* inside my head became, telling me to go and find out even more.

Through my research, I found that meditation was a big part of any kind of spiritual communication. Me meditate? Well, if I was going to find out what all of this was about, I knew I had to meditate.

At the time, I was working an average of twelve to fourteen hours a day, and it was not easy to come home to meditate after an exhausting day. It was really the last thing I wanted to do. I remember one night I came home after a very long day. It was around 1:00 A.M., and I had promised myself earlier that no matter how long I was at work that day, I *was* going to meditate when I got home. I sat on my bed, got comfortable, took some deep breaths, relaxed, and closed my eyes. I then started to focus and pay very close attention to any type of communication that might be coming my way from the other side. It wasn't too long before I *heard* something . . . not only that, I *felt* something!

It was the *sound* and the *sensation* of my head hitting the wall.

I had started to fall asleep, and fell backward, striking my head.

I decided not to meditate that night after all.

But I had come to believe that Heaven would give me the energy I needed to meditate—and Heaven did.

During meditation, the basic point is not to *think,* but to *receive.*

Easier said than done. When you're not supposed to do something, you automatically do it. I would relax and try to blank out everything in my mind, but then a thought would pop up about something that happened during the day. I would push it aside, and go blank again. Then another would sneak in. But I understood that this was normal, and slowly the more I practiced, the better I became.

I also read that we all have Spirit Guides. I have always believed in Guardian Angels, but a Spirit Guide? What are they?

I learned that these are spirits who have lived on Earth before, whereas angels have not. A guide could be a past family member, or even someone that one never knew, who is there to help us through life. The term "Spirit Guide" sounded strange and New Age-ish to me, but I knew we have family members watching over us (remember Uncle Edward?).

In my research, I happened across an audiotape which, through guided visualization, would help a person in meeting his or her guide. It sounded easy enough, so, going with that gut instinct again, I went ahead and purchased the tape.

That night, I made myself good and comfortable. Earlier, I had asked my guide (whoever that was) to please come and reveal who he or she was. I just wanted to make sure *everyone* was prepared. Placing my earphones on, I began listening to the tape. A female voice came on and began giving instructions on how to visualize a place in my mind. She said this was to be a wonderful and peaceful place, one of my own creation. While listening to her directions, soft music played in the background and I started feeling my energies begin to rise. I started to picture in my mind a large, comfortable room. There wasn't a lot in it, as I didn't want things to become too complicated, but a nice room nevertheless. In it, I envisioned a huge window where I had a view of a beautiful forest. The narrator instructed me to have a seat in my room, which I proceeded to do. I visualized myself sitting in a big old comfortable chair, one that you could easily sink into. While sitting in this chair, I was then told to see a door in front of me, which I did. The narrator said to mentally ask for my guide to come through it. "Okay, here goes," I thought, "let's see if anyone walks through the door."

To my surprise, there, in my mind, a person stood in front me.

Was I imagining all of this? I had no precognition of what to expect. I got up out of the chair and, as we both stood there, he introduced himself as "Andrew."

Andrew told me that he was a Spirit Guide, and had been my guide my entire life. I started to focus on Andrew to see exactly what he looked like. He was in his thirties, with long dark hair, and wore clothing that I would associate with colonial times. He had on a white shirt, which had baggy sleeves, and his pants were dark. I thought this was pretty cool, to say the least, and decided to go along with it. I asked Andrew to come in and sit in a chair beside me, and he did. As we began to talk, not only was I excited, but he was as well. He told me he had been waiting anxiously for the day when we would meet face to face, and had a hand in guiding me to it. Andrew also said that I was heading in the *right direction*. I said that was great, but where was the right direction? He said, "You'll see."

There was that "*You'll see*" again, but this time I not only heard it, I saw the person who was saying it!

I asked, "How do I know I'm not just imagining all of this?"

He assured me that I wasn't.

"If I'm not," I said, "give me some evidence that can prove this is real."

The challenge was on the table. Andrew looked up at me with a smile and said, "You will receive a reading and be told again that you have a gift. *This will be happening sooner than you think.*"

I said, "Okay, sounds good to me."

He smiled and then vanished before my eyes.

I was amazed at what had just taken place. I had met the voice I had been hearing for a long time, and now realized that it was coming from my guide, Andrew. Imagination or not, I had a buzz going all around my body as if I were on a caffeine high. It was hard to settle down that night to go to sleep, but I finally drifted off.

Did I really see and hear all this, or was it just an overactive imagination?

～

As I continued to develop with meditation, I would share all my experiences with Kathy. She, too, began reading and studying about spirituality, mediums, and the other side, as she was just as fascinated as I was. We both decided to see if we could make a private appointment with James Van Praagh. We met with his assistant, Cammy, but she informed us that James had a year-long waiting list. Even though there was a long wait, we told Cammy to place our names on the list. I started to think to myself that Andrew had said my confirmation was going to happen sooner than I think. Well, a year's wait for a reading was not what I called soon, so I thought maybe the confirmation would have to come from someone else.

Not long after that, I received a call at work from Cammy.

Cammy told me there had just been a cancellation with James, and asked if Kathy and I would be interested in taking this appointment. I was at work at the time, but I told her sure, both Kathy and I would be there. I drove home to pick up Kathy and we rushed through the Los Angeles traffic (a miracle in itself) to arrive just on time.

James sat us both down and after a few minutes of talking, started to receive spirits for us. The first person to come was our mother. It had been only a few months since her passing, and we were thrilled that she was able to speak to us so soon. One of the first things she wanted to do was wish me a happy birthday. My birthday was the first one to occur since her passing. Though usually apart on this day in recent years, she would always call me at the exact time I was born. This was something special we did between us.

She mentioned to Kathy she was watching her do her art work, and how proud she was of her talents. She also wanted to confirm she had also been watching over Kathy's cat. Since her cat was back in Virginia, this was a question that was on Kathy's mind earlier.

Then Mom brought up our dad. They had been married for over fifty years, and what was the first message for him? To cut his hair! Mom had always cut our father's hair, and after her passing, he decided not to let anyone else do it. As the months went by after her passing, his hair was growing longer and longer; eventually he had to wear it in a ponytail. It was very funny that she was bringing this up, since she would be the first one to get on him about the length of his hair. We had to make sure we told our father, because it would certainly confirm she was still with him.

Other confirmations came through, supporting our belief that she had been watching over us. Most people have this faith, but it is always good to hear certain confirmations to reinforce it. Other family members started to come through as well, as we excitedly received messages from all of them.

As the reading came to an end, James said something I had been wondering if I was going to hear. He said that I too had a gift, and that I would become a medium.

What I had heard from Andrew had come to pass, and sooner than I expected.

3

*Unwrapping
my gift*

I now knew I was on to something, and decided to go full
force with it. Though the visualization meditation was
good, I *knew* it had been only the first step—that I had
been, and was going to be, connecting with Spirit in other
ways. Day in and day out, I would come home after work
and persist with my meditations. I would pick out some
type of soft music, put my headphones on, and open myself up to Spirit. I would sit and receive any impressions
that came, and amazing things started happening to me.
With practice, I found myself able to feel a stronger presence of a spirit connecting to me. It was the same sensation one would have when sensing another person in a
room, but with a more acute feeling. Not only was I sensing one spirit, but at times many of them. The funny
thing was, I knew I had felt these impressions before! My
whole life, I had been experiencing these sensations, but I
didn't recognize them for what they were.

With the help of Andrew, I started to understand that
in my development I had to lay down guidelines for the
other side. Doing so would help me to have more control
over what I was doing and experiencing. I would ask my

mother to connect with me in a certain way, Andrew in another. I also gave out instructions to other family members on the other side—aunts uncles, even grandparents. I had many relatives over there, so I knew I would be receiving a lot of help from them. Not only was I able to intuit spirit presence, but also their emotions and personalities as well. With such a large family, there were many personalities for me to connect with.

As I continued enhancing my ability, I started to find myself able to separate my thoughts from theirs. Communicating with the other side is a lot different from communicating with someone here. Sometimes I would hear a voice from a spirit. Other times I would receive an image of something or someone that would flash before my eyes. I also was feeling what they were feeling. It took time and a lot of patience, but the more I practiced, the better I became.

A whole new world had opened up for me. I was finally communicating one-on-one with the other side!

With my gift becoming stronger, I knew I had to practice on someone—Kathy! I was still testing the waters, so she was more than willing to give me a hand. I had heard that other mediums found it difficult to speak with their family members who are on the other side. I knew during my development I would receive guidance from my mother, but this would come as a random thought, or a very strong feeling. It was time to see if I could actually give messages from her to someone else. The night before, I asked Mom if she would please come to us the next day so that I could give messages to Kathy. I asked her to come around 7:00 P.M. and to bring anyone else she liked. I thanked her in advance, and told her I loved her very much.

Kathy and I were both very excited the next night. Though we knew our mother was always around us, I wanted to relay some messages from her to Kathy. As we both sat in our living room, I opened myself up and started to sense my mother's presence. At first, I felt the love she was bringing and how she too was excited to be able to speak with us. I proceeded to ask Mom to tell me things she had seen Kathy do, as confirmations.

"Kathy, Mom is holding some flowers and smiling, and is thanking you," I said.

Kathy looked at me with a very happy smile. Preparing for tonight, she had mentally handed Mom flowers that day, telling her she hoped that she would enjoy them. Yes! A confirmation!

"She is also showing me a pie." Kathy had baked a pie that day and had invited Mom and the others over there to have some. Again another confirmation of something Kathy had done, yet about which I had no knowledge.

Keep in mind that anything you want to give to someone in Heaven, they can actually receive. Though it will not disappear from your hands, your thought of giving it makes it become real on the other side. It is not called Heaven for nothing!

The reading continued as more confirmations came through, not only for Kathy, but about other family members as well. My mother gave me information about my father and brothers to validate that she had been watching over them also.

Not only did Mom come through that night, but others surfaced as well, including Uncle Edward! There he was smiling at me again, happy that I was on the right path.

After awhile, I felt myself starting to get drained, so I knew it was time to wrap it up. We thanked everyone for coming that night and told them we looked forward to doing this again.

So there it was, my first reading. I don't think I have to tell you how excited we both were after it. We decided to go out to eat and celebrate with a good meal. At that time, and even today, I had to fast before giving a reading, and I was hungry, to say the least. Talking to spirits can do that to you, you know.

Once I got the hang of connecting spirits with Kathy, I was anxious to do it for others. I decided to go into chat rooms on the Internet, and see who might be seeking a reading. It usually didn't take long to find someone. I would relay the messages that I was hearing by typing them as fast as possible. People started to tell me how amazed they were with the information they received from their readings. I found myself getting just as excited about it as they did.

After awhile though, I found it distracting to try to convey loved ones' messages by typing them. Not only was information coming through during a reading, emotions were as well, and those were things I could not express by typing. By now, I had enough courage to take that leap and give readings to people one-on-one.

My friend Jeff was not really into this at the time. He found it all rather spooky. His grandmother, with whom he was extremely close, had passed and his mother, Shirley, was having a hard time dealing with this. I thought if I could connect with his grandmother, it would help begin the healing process for both of them. Although skeptical, Jeff agreed. He would welcome any message that would help both of them.

As Jeff sat anxiously in front of me, his grandmother came through right away, with a great deal of love. She expressed that she had been watching over him and his family and wanted to assure everyone that she was still around. She also commented on the fact that she knew how hard a time Shirley had been having in dealing with her passing and wanted to help with this.

If Jeff had been skeptical, his mother was even more so. Not brought up in an environment that embraced spirituality, she had serious reservations. Like many others, she would believe it only if it was demonstrated to her. I asked Jeff's grandmother to give me some confirmations that would connect with his mother, helping her with the healing process.

"Jeff, your grandmother is telling me she saw your mother looking at flags today."

Since his mother was three thousand miles away, he had no way of knowing if this was correct or not.

"She is also telling me that the wedding is going to take place and that she was with your mom and aunt while they were discussing this."

"There is not going to be a wedding now," he said.

Jeff knew his cousin had planned to get married, but had called it off. I thought to myself, was I hearing this wrong? His grandmother repeated herself again.

I said, "You may not know this, but your mother will. There is going to be a wedding."

Once again, Jeff had no idea, but he said he would check on it. His grandmother gave other information about the family and some of their problems. She reassured him she was all right and trying to help them in every way she could. She loved them all dearly and was always with the family. I could tell this meant a lot to Jeff, and he called his mother soon afterward. She had been on a trip to upstate New York visiting her family and had some news for Jeff. You guessed it—his cousin was in fact getting married and Shirley had purchased a decorative new flag for their home. This was information that Jeff had no knowledge of. It was concrete proof for them that his grandmother was watching over them.

I especially like this in a reading. It's okay to be skeptical, but when I give information that only the two parties could possibly know, that clinches it.

As news got out to our other friends that I could communicate with the other side, Kathy started to arrange readings for them. They would come to our home or I would give them a reading over the phone, and their response was overwhelming. Some people would ask me, how is it possible to do a reading over the phone? They think their loved ones would have to come to me through the phone lines. Not at all. If someone on Earth can connect with another person by dialing a seven-digit phone number, *Heaven* has no problem in finding me.

Working in Hollywood was taking up most of my time. People have the misconception that showbiz is all glamorous. Believe me, it's not. Most people in it work very, very long hours. I didn't mind that at the time, but I had to come to the realization that in order to continue with my spiritual work I would have to say goodbye to my Hollywood career.

This was not the easiest thing to do.

I was making more money than I ever had and also saw great opportunities ahead. I always felt lucky having this job, but as time passed, I realized that it was supposed to be only temporary. I had achieved one dream, only to find out that it was leading to something bigger. I *knew* what I was supposed to do, and I had to *trust* that voice I had heard on my first day of the job.

So it was goodbye showbiz, hello Patrick Mathews, the spiritual medium.

4

My field of dreams

Word about my abilities started to spread outside of our circle. I would receive calls and email from people around the country who wanted to connect with their loved ones. Clients to whom I gave readings would tell their family and friends, and they, too, would want to have a session with me. All this had a snowball effect. To my surprise, people not only wanted to have a reading, but as the list grew, had to wait a month or two to get one. I wanted to help as many people as possible, but knew that I couldn't push myself too hard. It can drain you of energy to receive information from the other side, so I had to learn to pace myself.

Kathy suggested I should give a public demonstration. There were a lot of curious people out there—she thought this would be a great way to make people aware of what it was I did. With the help of a few of our friends spreading the word, as well as support from a local bookstore, we arranged a demonstration of spiritual communication.

When the night of the event came, I was really pumped up. I was ready to share the other side with an audience, and confirm that their loved ones were still very much around them.

Kathy and I arrived early to make sure everything was properly set up, then went into a side room to relax and gather our thoughts before the demonstration was to begin. Even from this separate room, we could feel the air becoming charged as people began arriving with the anticipation of hearing from a loved one in spirit. When it was time to begin, Kathy and I entered the room. To my surprise, we were greeted by loud applause. We were both very humbled by the audiences' enthusiastic welcome.

I started the lecture by explaining what I do and how I receive messages. Both Kathy and I answered questions from the audience. Kathy had gained a lot of knowledge about communications with those on the other side from studying the many readings I had done. The kindness and compassion she has toward others makes her a natural speaker.

After the questions and answers, I started a meditation for the audience to help level all the energies in the room before beginning the readings. During the silent part of the meditation, something unusual happened. I started receiving a message from Spirit but it was not for anyone in the audience, it was for *me*. Images, words, and feelings started to flood my mind, among them were:

- Me as a young boy, awakened in the middle of the night, having the spirit of my Uncle Edward give me a message for the family.

- While growing up, constantly *feeling* the presence of spirits around me, but not understanding at the time what they were.

- Being *pulled* to move to California in order to have events unfold in my life, which placed me on my life's path.

- Reminded of being told "*not to get too comfortable with my Hollywood job.*"

- It being said that *I too had a gift*, and would be using it in order to help people.

- Finally finding myself *giving in to my gut instinct* and that *voice* I had been hearing all along.

- Leaving all the plans and dreams I had once had for myself, and *changing* my life and future to something that, at one time, I never dreamed possible.

A light bulb went off in my head, and *it finally all connected*. I had been receiving signs my entire life. Each event, by itself, didn't make sense, but *together* they formed a complete picture. The picture was where I was that night, and what I would be doing for the rest of my life.

There I was, Patrick Mathews, sitting in front of an audience of people, about to connect them with their loved ones on the other side.

It all came together just as it had for Ray in Field of Dreams.

At that special moment, my loved ones in spirit had flooded me with all these messages as *my personal confirmation from above.*

It took everything I had to hold back the tears.

Even at my age, you have to be cool.

Part II

❧

Conversations with the other side

The following section explains what it is like to communicate with those on the other side, and what types of messages our loved ones in spirit wish to convey.

5

Communicating
with spirits

I have been asked many times if communicating with spirit is the same as talking with people?

That would be nice, but communicating with those on the other side is very different from how we do it here. When giving someone a reading, I would love to hear:

"Hi, I'm Robert. That's my wife, Betty, you're talking to. I passed away in March, 2003, from a heart attack. I have two children, Bobby Jr. and Sharon, my dog's name is Pete. I worked as a teacher, and I loved to dance."

But unfortunately it doesn't work that way.

When I am speaking with spirits, their messages will consist of information that will come through to me in several ways, most commonly by clairaudience, clairvoyance, and clairsentience. Now before I confuse you further, the following are examples of what I'm talking about.

Clairaudience

This is a French word meaning "clear hearing." Hearing a message from a spirit does not necessarily mean with my physical ear, but with my inner ear. This would be similar to what one hears when thinking to oneself.

When a spirit communicates using clairaudience, it is usually at a very rapid pace. At times, I will hear whole words, at other times, only parts of a word. I always enjoy communicating with a spirit who would have been very vocal here, or what you might call a "loud mouth." It makes it a lot easier to hear them through clairaudience.

Tom made an appointment with me to contact his brother David, who passed from a motorcycle accident. Even though he knew his brother was still with him, Tom wanted some reassurance. When David came in, he was a very vocal fellow. Throughout the reading, he gave Tom numerous confirmations, but there were also a few surprises.

"David wants me to remind you of the 'Moon.' Are you, or was he, into astronomy?"

Tom looked puzzled.

"No," said Tom.

"Okay," I said. "He's being kind of stern, while laughing at the same time, and keeps telling me 'Moon,' and is connecting this with both of you."

Tom pondered it for a second, then, shaking his head, replied, "I can't think of any kind of a moon thing."

I continued. "I want you to know David's laughing really hard now, and this is what he's telling me, 'You . . . he . . . moon . . . mooning.' Wait a minute, I get it now . . . he's telling me you guys mooned people!"

Tom mouth dropped. "Oh my god, I can't believe it. The night before David's accident, we were joking around with some friends, and both of us flashed our butts at them. We did moon them!"

We were all laughing at that one. I was just glad David decided to get that message across with words—not pictures.

Clairvoyance

This means "clear seeing." Clairvoyance is when a spirit will actually show me images. Receiving these images would be similar to those seen in a daydream. I'm not necessarily seeing them with my physical eyes, but with my mind's eye.

I once gave a reading to a woman named Carol. During the session, her mother, who had passed, came in and told me she overheard a conversation Carol had just had with a girlfriend before her appointment with me. She said the conversation was of a spiritual nature, consisting of talk about religions, Jesus, and Mary. Carol thought it was amazing that her mother was standing right there listening to the conversation! Everything I had said was right, except she didn't recall talking about Mary.

"Hmmm. Okay, let's see If I can get this straight then," I said. "Your mother is showing me religious articles. To me, this means you were talking religion with your friend."

"Yes, you're right, we were talking religion," Carol said

"She is also showing me an imagine of Jesus. So I know that you must had been talking about him, too," I said.

"That's right, we were talking about Jesus."

"And your mother keeps showing me the Madonna, so to me, this means you were discussing Mary as well."

Carol thought for a moment, and burst out laughing. "No, we were not talking about the Madonna, Mary—but about Madonna, the singer!"

Go figure.

Clairsentience

This means "clear feeling." These messages will come through as feelings—the feeling of a spirit's personality, their sadness, happiness, love, gender, age, even how they passed. A spirit will usually use clairsentience to emphasize a point they're trying to get across, as with the following example.

Tina was very anxious to speak with her son Philip, who passed away at the age of eight from an irregular heart valve complication. The passing came quickly and as a total surprise. During the reading, Philip brought through many confirmations for his mother and the entire family. At one point in the reading, Tina asked what Philip was doing on the other side. Philip decided to not show me or tell me, but let me feel it.

"Tina, I keep feeling as if I am falling, not a long distance, but a short one. Did Philip used to fall down a lot?"

"Not more than any other boy, I guess," she said.

"This is strange. You asked what he was doing, and all he keeps doing is letting me feel that I am falling. Let me see what he is talking about."

At that moment, the feeling of falling stopped and changed to a floating sensation.

"Tina, Philip is now letting me feel he is flying. This should mean something to you."

Tina, through tears of joy, said, "Yes! Philip used to tie a towel around his neck like a cape and act like Superman. He would jump off our porch with his hands raised up as if he were going to fly. The porch was only about three feet off the ground, so we knew he wouldn't hurt himself. As soon as he landed on the ground, he would run back up and do it again."

"Well, he wants you to know he can really fly now, and this is what he is doing!" I said. "He also wants you to know he has a real cape!"

When communicating with those on the other side, it is always their choice of how they will want to make the connection, but it's usually a combination of all of the above. Because our loved ones are at a higher level or a higher vibration, the information they convey comes to me very rapidly. My role is to first receive this information as quickly as they are giving it, decipher the message they are trying to get across, and then deliver it.

I guess you could call me a *spirit walkie talkie!*

5

Life changing messages?

What type of messages do loved ones want to convey from Heaven? Well, it really depends on the person receiving the reading and what they may or may not need to hear.

First, let me start by saying that I have no control over what a spirit will tell me. Though no two readings are alike, the common factor in every reading is that your loved ones want to convey they are still very much alive and watching over you. That message is very meaningful, and should be taken to heart, but I also insist a spirit give information that will hit home for the person being read. Usually, the spirit will bring through personal information about themselves, the person I am reading, and other members of the family. Names, places, and life events are other things that will be mentioned as well. The messages may be as complex as asking forgiveness for a wrong that was done or as simple as saying they saw the person picking flowers that morning. The meaning in it all is to show they are still with you and can prove it.

At a reading, one should *never* go in expecting to hear an *exact* message from someone on the other side. By doing so, you may be limiting all the other wonderful information that does come through by the spirit.

A good example of this is when I once gave a reading to a woman named Judy. Judy came to see me in hopes of connecting with her mother. She told me she knew her mother had a message for her, and she was ready to receive it. I started the session.

"Your mother is letting me feel as if she passed by natural causes, a very slow death. She passed with cancer."

"Yes," Judy replied.

"Your mother is now taking that feeling away from me. Please understand, she was only letting me feel her passing for the benefit of identification, but she no longer feels this way. She wants me to convey this to you loud and clear!"

"That's nice to hear." Judy said.

I said. "Okay, she is also stating you have a younger sister."

"Yes," Judy said.

I said, "Please let her know Mom is just fine. She wants me to thank you both for all that you did for her. She also wants you to know this does not go unnoticed by her or by God."

Although this was just the start of the reading, I thought things were going great. Her mother was coming in strong, but I sensed Judy being a little hesitant, which I attributed to nerves.

"Do you work outside?" I asked.

"No," Judy answered.

"Hmmm, your mom is telling me that you work outside," I said.

"No, I work in an office," Judy replied.

"That's strange, she keeps showing me you outside working."

"I do like to garden."

"I see, but no, that's not it. She is saying she saw you *working* outside."

"I really have no idea what she is talking about," Judy said.

"Okay, I'll ask her to go to the next thing," I said.

I know that during a reading a person's mind is going a mile minute, trying to make a connection to the messages. Being in this state, sometimes he or she will emphatically get what I call *psychic amnesia*. I could tell them that they are married, and they will state they are not. After the reading, once having a chance to settle down, comes "Oh, that's right, I am married!" It happens, so I usually just go on to the next thing, knowing it will make sense later, but at times the spirit does not want to go on, and will just stick with it until the confirmation is made.

"Well, it looks as if your mom still wants to get this confirmation across. She is telling me you were working outside recently, and you didn't want to."

Judy looked puzzled—then all of a sudden her facial expression changed, and she made the connection.

"Oh, that's right. I work in an office that needed to be exterminated. I am really sensitive to the smell of pesticides, so I had to work outdoors for a while, until my office aired out. I really wasn't dressed properly, and was pretty uncomfortable."

I was glad the connection was finally made.

I said, "Well, your mom was there watching you, and was also trying to cool you off, she is telling me."

Judy shook her head and smiled.

"You want to know if your mom hears you, she is telling me, and the answer is . . . every single word. You also want to know if she is helping you, and of course she is, any way that she is able."

With that, Judy seemed to sit up with anticipation.

"Have you noticed a strange sound that is coming from a radio? She is saying she's been playing with one."

"I was just banging on my clock radio this morning. It was making this loud, hissing sound, and I was wondering what was causing it!"

"Well, it's Mom, so blame her! She wants you to know she is always around you, giving you signs, so just continue to notice them."

After many more validations and messages from her mother, the reading came to a close.

Although smiling, I could sense Judy was a little disappointed. I asked her if she was not happy with the reading. She replied that she was happy, but the one thing she was hoping to hear did not come through. I asked her what it was.

Judy said, "The winning lottery numbers. My mother and I always played the lottery, and I had asked before I came for her to tell me what they were going to be. That is what I really wanted to hear from her."

You have got to be kidding me, I thought. My mouth must have dropped. Here, Judy's mother came in and gave her many wonderful confirmations and messages. Not only was she still watching over Judy and the rest of her family, the fact of the matter was that she, too, was alive and well, and not suffering any longer with cancer. That was all good and fine, but the only thing Judy was waiting to hear throughout the whole reading was some winning lottery numbers.

While waiting to hear that one certain thing, all the other information Judy heard went in one ear and out the other. This was why her mother was so adamant about all of the validations she had stated. She was trying to break through the barrier Judy had placed on herself.

It's very much like a child who has his or her heart set on a bike for Christmas. The child runs down on Christmas morning, tearing past all the trains, dolls, tea sets, and other goodies to find the bike. Instead of enjoying what is there, he or she has blinders on that direct them to that one thing.

When having a reading, my suggestion is to be open to any messages you may receive, just as long as they are *specific enough* that they apply only to you.

Making a connection with the other side is a miracle in and of itself. Every piece of information is a gift, and should be taken to heart, but if you are looking for your loved ones in spirit to give you winning lottery numbers, as Judy did, or for them to tell you how to become rich, you will be disappointed. Will they help guide you through certain situations? Yes. But the bottom line is, we're the ones responsible for our lives here, and with that responsibility, comes success as well as failure. Again, this is how we learn and grow—through making our own decisions. Though the messages the spirits give may not give you all the answers to your life questions, it should be enough to confirm and prove to you that they are always with you.

Isn't that really the most important gift they can give?

Part III

❧

Lessons from heaven

In the following section, I want to share with you a few of the many readings I have given throughout the years. Though no two readings are ever alike, (each is as different as the individual to whom I am speaking, here and on the other side), some have had a tendency to be truly memorable, each holding a lesson from which to learn.

7

A child's love never dies

One of the most difficult types of passing a person would ever have to experience would be that of losing a child.

As we live our lives, we perceive that one day we will experience the passing of our grandparents and eventually our parents. Having knowledge of these realities of life does not make them any easier to go through once they occur, but it does help us to mentally prepare ourselves for when and if they do.

When a parent loses a child, this is something that is usually never anticipated, nor is it prepared for. This type of loss seems to break our rules for life, and usually places a person in a state of deep heartache and grief.

I feel very blessed when I am able to help a parent make a connection to a child who has passed, and one of the most touching was for a woman named Jillian.

Jillian felt she was on the verge of suicide because of the recent loss of her son. Desperate for help, she was looking on the internet for grief counseling. She didn't intend to look up mediums, but for some reason, my name came up in her search. Although far from her original intention, she looked up my web page. She felt something was telling her that this was the right thing to do and I was the person to contact. Making an appointment to see me was a last-ditch effort for her.

The day of Jillian's appointment came. She flew into Los Angeles and drove straight to my office from the airport. Sitting her down, I told her to relax and that we'd see who might have flown in with her, trying to joke to relieve some of the pressure she must have felt. Not knowing who she wanted to contact, I explained how I worked, and we began the session.

"I'm getting an older woman wanting to talk to you," I said.

Jillian just sat there, motionless.

"A grandmother," I said. "She's telling me that she had not been close to you, but she wants you to know she watches over you."

"That is very nice to hear!" Jillian replied. "I knew only one of my grandmothers, and we were not very close. She lived far away from my family and passed away when I was a child, so I never really got to know her."

"Well, she knows you very well, she says!"

I could see that message made Jillian relax a little more.

"Your grandmother is telling me although she would love to continue to chat with you, someone else wants to talk. You have a son on the other side, yes?"

That did it—this was the door she longed to have opened.

"Oh my gosh," Jillian said. "Is my son here?"

She started to shake with anticipation.

With that, the spirit of a young boy came through. When I told this to Jillian, she started to tear up.

"He's telling me to give you lots and lots of love," I said. "I can't even begin to tell you how excited he is!"

Excited was an understatement! He kept moving around and I had to tell him to keep still, as I had to focus on him in one place. He would stand in one area for a few seconds, then run around the room to another location. I could sense he had an enormous life energy and that it was still with him. His love for his family was overwhelming.

Being able to feel those kinds of emotions from Spirit is one of my rewards of doing this work.

Losing a child has to be one of the most painful losses a person can have, but the circumstances of that loss in some cases can make it almost unbearable.

"Your son is talking about his passing. He is now giving me the sensation of my throat closing . . . so I can tell he couldn't breath when he passed . . . did he choke or drown?"

"Yes," she said, and with that, started to cry.

"He wants you to know that he went to Heaven quickly, and that it didn't hurt."

Jillian let out a sigh of relief and began to cry even harder.

Her son Todd had died a few months earlier in their backyard. Their dog had been chained up around a tree, and the chain somehow had gotten wrapped around Todd's neck. It happened in a matter of seconds.

During the reading, Todd was emphatic that no one should feel guilty. He wanted his mother to know that, believe it or not, it had been his time to go. Although it had seemed like a horrible accident, he told her no one should blame themselves, it was simply in his plan.

"Todd wants you to know that he is okay, he is still with you, and is still a part of the family," I said. "Todd is talking about a root planted by the window?"

"Oh my gosh," Jillian exclaimed again. "Todd and I rooted a plant and put it on the kitchen window sill so the sun could shine on it most of the day."

"Great," I said. "He also says someone is standing at the same window and they see him, they see him now."

Jillian thought for a moment, then said no, but Todd was insistent on this.

"'Yes, Mom, yes,' he is telling me to tell you. They have seen him also in the mirror."

Still unsure, I told her to hang onto this information and it might make sense later.

After the reading, when her husband Dan listened to the tape of the session, he heard this part and exclaimed, "That's me!" Dan hadn't told Jillian, but almost every day, he would stand at that window and look outside. Several times he thought he had seen Todd, but hesitated to share this with his wife, thinking it was just his imagination. He knew now that it wasn't. No one else knew he had stood at that particular window and had seen Todd several times. Jillian and Dan found out later that Todd's older brother Randy had also had encounters with Todd. While looking in the mirror he had seen Todd in the reflection, but had not told his mom or dad.

"Todd is saying you need to eat! He is being very strong on this message," I said.

Jillian wiped the tears, smiled and shook her head. These were his words verbatim to her before he passed. Jillian had a stomach disorder and never wanted to eat. Even though he was just a little boy, this always worried Todd.

"Music at the funeral," I said. "Todd is saying there was something wrong, but he's okay about it. Someone made a big deal about the music, but that's all right, it's fine."

Jillian let out a sigh of relief.

She told me. "Todd didn't like church music because when he sang out loud in church, his friends would make fun of him."

Some of her family had wanted traditional music at the funeral, but Jillian didn't. After a lot of discussion on this with family members, Jillian had agreed to play one of Todd's favorite songs, along with the traditional music. Todd had a wide taste in music. Jillian remembered that he liked the song that says, "*God must have spent a little more time with you,*" and she chose that.

"He's telling me there was other music that he liked, which *you didn't play,*" I said. "But it's okay."

Jillian laughed and told me that he did like a few heavy metal tunes but she didn't think they would be appropriate.

I assured her he was all right with that, as well.

"Two shirts!" I said. "He keeps talking about his two shirts at the funeral."

Jillian put her hand over her mouth with excitement.

"We did have a discussion about his shirts and which one he would wear," Jillian said. "He loved wrestling, but he also loved this Mustang shirt and we didn't know which to put on him."

Jillian was excited with this confirmation.

"He's telling me he liked them both and you made it work!"

"Yes, yes, we decided to put both on him, because the wrestling shirt was buttoned down and the Mustang shirt could be seen underneath!" she said, while sitting straightforward in her chair.

I could see that hearing from Todd was bringing Jillian back to life. Todd had a lot of things still to tell his mom; things that would assure her he was still part of the family.

"He's telling me that 'Mom put the ornament on the tree,'" I said.

Knowing Christmas had just gone by, I didn't think this was the most original point of evidence I could give her, but I just convey what I hear.

"He's telling me this is very important; that it's unusual," I said.

Jillian excitedly replied, "I know exactly what he's talking about! Two weeks before he died, Todd had worked on a Christmas ornament at school, and his teacher brought it over on Christmas Eve. She explained how excited Todd was when he was making it, and thought we would want to have it. My husband instantly placed it on the tree, but I had him take it down. Knowing this was the last art project Todd had worked on was just too much for me to take. But after thinking long and hard about it, *something* made me put it back up."

I replied. "He wants you to know that it was his gift to you, and *he* was the one to nudge you to place it back on the tree."

Jillian replied through smiles and tears, "I will cherish it for the rest of my life."

The next part of the reading shows that love is concrete—and with it, all things are possible.

"Hmmm, Todd wants you to know that it wasn't his 'last art project.' He's now talking about a drawing," I said. "A special drawing he left for you."

All of a sudden, Jillian became elated as she bent over and pulled out a drawing from her purse. Holding the picture with shaking hands, she explained to me what it was.

After Todd's passing, Jillian had not been able to work for months. She had tried to talk herself into thinking that Todd was only hiding from her, not dead.

For her family's sake, Jillian decided to go ahead with Christmas, but bought Christmas gifts for Todd as well. She realized she was in denial, but this was her way of getting through the pain and heartache she was experiencing.

One afternoon, Jillian started thoroughly cleaning the house for the upcoming holidays. While working through an area in the kitchen, she came across her crystal candy dish. Removing the lid to dust inside, she noticed a folded piece of paper in it. Unfolding it, to her amazement, she recognized Todd's handwriting. On the piece of paper was a drawing (stickman fashion) of her and Todd. He was standing next to her with blue tears coming down his face. At the very top of the drawing, he had written, "*Mom, I want you to feel much better, I love you.*"

Todd had always shown his artwork to her, as Jillian would make a big deal about it. This would always make Todd feel proud. Yet, neither she nor anyone in the family had ever seen this drawing before. She knew it wasn't something from the past because Jillian always kept a neat house, especially in the kitchen where she spent so much of her time. With this message, she now had confirmation where this drawing came from; it was a gift from Todd.

It's amazing to me that not only can those on the other side relay messages through thought and voice, but they can leave inanimate objects for us to find as well. We can never fully comprehend the power of love, or how these things happen, but we can look at the evidence, find it is real, and be grateful for all the signs that come our way of their continuing life.

Jillian had heard a lot of fantastic things that day, and came to the understanding that Todd was still her son, a part of the family, and that neither he nor his love would ever die.

8

Reuniting the family from the other side

Just as we learn lessons with classmates in school, our families play a similar role. They are our classmates in this school we call *life*. As in school, we sometimes get along well with our classmates, other times not. The same holds true with family members.

When a member of a family passes, several things can happen:

A divided family can come together.

A divided family can stay divided.

A close family can become divided.

A close family can stay together.

I have found in many readings I have given that spirits from the other side will try to bring closeness back to their families.

This is of the utmost importance to those on the other side.

Samantha came to me wanting to make a connection with her parents, Monica and Alan. She loved them both very dearly and was hoping to gain some guidance from them. She got what she came for.

As we both sat down to begin the session, I was pleasantly surprised by the fragrance of roses. It was not due to any perfume Samantha was wearing, nor were there any flowers around the room. I knew this was the way Monica wanted to begin the session.

"Your mother is here and is bringing you some roses, and she tells me she has been leaving flower scents around your home."

"Oh yes," Samantha cried out. "I have been smelling flowers and that reminded me of mother. She loved to garden."

"Well she still does garden and tells me you did, as well," I said.

"I haven't done it in years, but yes, we would garden together."

"She's been leaving flower scents for you as a sign that she and your father are still around and are watching over you . . . over the family, she says."

"I'm so happy to hear that!" replied Samantha.

I could tell that Samantha was happy to be speaking with her mother and was anxiously waiting to hear more.

"Your mother is saying the number five to me; I usually connect this with an anniversary or birthday. Is there one in May, or the fifth of a month?"

"I don't know, I don't think so," said Samantha.

"Hmmm, now she is holding up her hand and showing me five fingers. It should make a connection with you."

Samantha sat there, and I could tell that she was concentrating on what the five meant. Silently, I asked Monica to give me more.

"She's not letting this go and wants to be stubborn about this," I said, laughing. "She is showing me a five, and this has something to do with a birthday."

With that Monica showed me five birthday cakes.

"Wait . . . birthdays," I said. "Oh, she has five children."

Samantha shouted, surprised, "Five, yes!"

It's funny how a spirit will want to convey a message sometimes. With that I felt the spirit of a man wanting to connect. It was Samantha's father.

"Your father is also here, and wants to send love to you and your family. I am feeling a quick passing with them both; they were in an accident."

"Yes," said Samantha.

"They both were in the car, they passed over together," I said.

Samantha's voice was shaking as she answered, "Yes."

"Well, know from your dad that he and your mother are still together, even on the other side."

"They were married for forty-eight years," Samantha said.

"Yes, they were and are soul mates," I said.

"Your father also wants you to know that they felt no pain with their passing."

"I prayed that they passed quickly," Samantha replied.

"Here one minute and in Heaven the next, your father is telling me."

Samantha smiled because this message brought her comfort.

One day, Samantha's parents were making a simple run down to the corner grocery store to pick up a few items. While waiting at a traffic light, a tractor trailer coming from the opposite direction had lost control and slammed into them. They both passed away instantly.

"They passed awhile ago, around five or six years?" I asked.

"Six," replied Samantha

"Okay," I said. "Please make sure you thank everyone for their prayers. It means so much to both of them, he's telling me."

"I will make sure I do that," Samantha said.

"I can also tell your father was a well-educated man here," I said.

"Oh, you can say that again."

"He is showing me a bank; was this his occupation?"

"Not really."

"Hmmm, he shows me money in the bank . . . oh, I see. He's telling me your family was and is financially secure."

"Yes, very," Samantha replied.

"But there are concerns about the money now, and this has to do with you and your other family members, he is telling me."

"There are some problems," Samantha said sheepishly.

"Oh, oh. Your mother wants to talk about you and your other siblings," I said.

"I know where this is going," Samantha stated.

"She is showing me children, you and the others, and seems to be pulling everyone apart. Your family is separated, correct?"

Samantha said, "Yes."

"I'm not only talking distance, but also relationships. This is what your mother is telling me."

"Yes, she is correct."

"She is also saying the separation has to do with the money they left you."

"Yes," said Samantha. "This is true."

Samantha came from a wealthy family of three brothers and one sister—she being the middle child. When both parents passed, they stated in their will that all assets be divided equally among the children, but when it came time to receive the inheritance, the problems began. Some felt they deserved more than the others, and their bickering over the estate had turned Samantha's siblings against each other.

A once-close family was now torn apart. Instead of grief for their loss, greed had taken over.

"Your father is telling me you have not talked to some of your brothers for quite a while."

"Correct," Samantha said.

"Well, you know that you and the rest of your family have to heal your relationship. It is important that you do so," I said. "This is why your parents are bringing up all of this. They want you to know they are quite concerned."

"Some of us are communicating with each other, and some not," said Samantha.

"Your father wants you to know you all need to come to terms with this. You have to understand that on the other side, they see the bigger picture. What matters is not the material things you have, but more the thoughts and feelings you have for one another, for these are what comprise our souls."

Samantha was sitting on the edge of her chair, with both hands gripping at the seat cushions.

"But some of them won't talk to me," Samantha said.

"Your mother is telling me you tried, but gave up. Is this true?"

"Yes, I just figured what's the point? Why should I be the one to do all the work?" Samantha said.

"Well, just do your part. It will be up to the others to accept your offer, but at least you tried. I think also you may be surprised at how the others will respond now. Your father is telling me that although he had more boys, you were always most like him, the 'strong one.' Now you must act like the leader."

"I have been thinking about this for a while. What should I do?" Samantha said, now more at ease with the conversation taking place.

I replied, "Send a card or perhaps give them a call. But at least give it your best shot. Your father also says that you are the most stubborn of the bunch and you can use that strong will for the good of the family."

Smiling, Samantha shook her head and said, "Okay, I will."

"Your mother is mentioning that one brother has a birthday coming up. Please tell him 'Happy Birthday' from both of them."

"Yes, my brother William's birthday is at the end of the month."

"She says this might just be the right place and time to start."

The one thing Samantha's parents wanted to get across was that even though families may argue with each other from time to time, the most important thing is forgiveness and love.

Some people look at the value of love in dollars and cents. They feel the more money they receive, the more they must be loved. The true value of love does not come from a checkbook, but from the heart. With that, the true legacy of any family is how they can forgive each other and come together to help one another.

Forgiveness and love are truly the most important tools that we possess. By using them, we are not only helping others, but ourselves as well.

9

Painful passings —why?

Physical death can be painful and, depending on the circumstance, even cruel. We often wonder—if God is so loving, why then does he *allow* someone to pass with a long-suffering illness.

With the passing of his father, Robert had struggled with this question for years. He and his wife Terry had come to see me in the hope of talking to his father and finding some answers.

It was a cold and rainy Monday, and I had only one reading left to do that day. Terry was in the reception area and I came out to greet her. I asked if she was alone, because I had been told it was to be a reading for two. Robert came in from parking the car, and Terry smiled and said her better half had arrived. We went into my office and I explained what I do and what they could expect. They both listened intently, and I then started the reading.

"Let's see who's here," I said.

I didn't have to wait long because at that moment I felt a strong male presence burst into the room.

I looked at Robert and said, "Your father is coming in first, and I can tell you, he is coming in very strong."

Robert smiled, as his wife grabbed and held his hand in hers.

"I can feel he had a very slow passing," I said.

"Yes," replied Robert.

"With cancer," I said.

"Yes," Robert blurted out, excited. "He. . . ."

"Let him tell me, Robert," I said.

I could see that he wanted to tell me about it, but I prefer those on the other side to tell me first.

Robert relaxed and smiled.

"I keep hearing Fred or Frank."

"My dad's name is Frank," Robert said.

"Frank is coming through as if he has something to prove and keeps telling me how strong he is. He wants you to realize that he is not in any way, shape, or form the man you saw lying in that bed."

Robert bowed his head down to hide his emotions, which were now coming through.

"Frank is someone I would refer to as a 'man's man'. He never showed a lot of emotion with you," I said.

Robert now was doing everything he could to hold back the tears.

"He wants me to tell you something you need to hear from him . . . 'I love you.'"

That was it. Upon hearing those words, Robert broke down and started to cry. Though he knew his father did love him, it had never been said out loud. Frank was raised "old school," having been taught that men do not show or express their emotion, but they were both showing and expressing it now.

"Your father also wants you to tell the family how healthy he now is, and it's important never to think of him the way he was at the end."

In the past, Frank was always in good physical shape. Being a construction worker, there were times when even the younger fellows found it hard to keep up with him. Everyone liked Frank, and often he and his crew would go out for a beer after a hard day's work. Things started changing when at day's end Frank felt too tired to go out and instead headed straight home. Being the strong guy that he was, he didn't even tell his wife that he didn't feel like his old self any more. It was not until the day he found it hard to get out of bed that he told his wife something was wrong. With her insistence, they went to the hospital.

After what seemed like an eternity, the results of his tests came back. Their worse fears were realized. Frank was told he had cancer—it was inoperable, and he had less than a handful of months to live.

Even with such devastating news, Frank showed no emotion when he told the news to his family, since he did not want to be a burden to anyone. That was Frank. As time went by, his condition deteriorated, and he lost an enormous amount of weight. It was hard for him to let go of his stubbornness, but eventually he had to, allowing his family to take care of him once he became bedridden. It wasn't easy for his family, especially his sons, to see their father becoming so dependent, but they did everything to keep a brave face on and to make Frank as comfortable as possible.

This was not the way Frank had wanted to pass. He had always told his wife that he wanted to go quickly and not be dependent on anyone. He wondered what had he done to deserve this? He'd been a good husband and father, but just didn't understand why God was doing this to him.

I continued, "Frank wants you to know one important thing. He is *now* very proud of the way he passed and feels fortunate to have gone through it."

Robert looked puzzled, knowing how much his father had hated being sick.

"How is that possible?" he asked. "Dad despised being as helpless as he was."

I paused to let Frank answer.

"He is showing me that he is proudly wearing the illness as a medal on his chest. He tells me by going through this type of passing, he was given a wonderful opportunity. By allowing you and your family to help him, all the love you gave him is now a part of him, a part of his soul. But it also works both ways. By you and your family wanting to help him unconditionally the way you did, your souls grew as well."

Robert and Terry both started to cry, and with all that emotion coming from them, I started to tear up, myself.

I further explained to the couple that even in passing we are here to learn lessons. Depending on the situation, we can receive love from each other as well as give it. It is through those times of great need that one has the chance for both learning and love. It is not a punishment from God, but a gift of learning and an opportunity for enhancing our souls. *We are all unique, with unique lives, but our passings are also unique lessons—a final gift on Earth for us to use or share.*

Robert thanked me and couldn't wait to go home and tell the rest of the family. He said he now understood what a gift it was to have his strong father reach out to them for help. He always felt that although it was hard to see his father that way, he actually had felt closer to him during those last weeks than he ever had before. He became a better person for it.

He knew his father would explain everything and make it right, just as he had done in life.

10

Suicide and forgiveness

Be it for love, financial, or medical reasons, some who have felt an extreme sense of loss, depression, or confusion take their own lives. Is this the right thing to do?

Absolutely not.

In school, why are there lessons? The answer is simple, so that we may learn and enhance our minds.

You may not remember now, but when in school, I'm sure there were many difficult times and tasks you encountered while learning different lessons. There may have been things you didn't understand and struggled with. But by pushing yourself, your mind, you persevered.

Let me ask you, what would have happened if you had given up and decided to, let's say, not learn to read? How would your life be different?

- You certainly would not have this book in your hand right now.

- You wouldn't be able to drive, because you would not be able to read road signs.

- You couldn't write your thoughts or wishes to anyone.

- You couldn't even write a check, or use an ATM.

- You couldn't use a computer, type, or even write a note to someone.

By continuing to learn to read, by going through all the tests and problems, you expanded your mind. You grew, and by accomplishing this particular goal, for the rest of your life you have all the rewards that come from learning that lesson.

The same holds true for your soul. We are given situations and problems in this life so that our own spirits can also learn and grow. Without these lessons, we are stagnant, we stop advancing, stop learning. The fact of the matter is, the more our souls gain from all of life's experiences, the closer we become to God.

It is up to us how close to God we want to be.

I know that all of us have gone through some hard, and even tragic times in our lives, but by going through them, haven't we come out stronger? I would think most of us have. The one thing to remember is it's not only our minds that have become stronger, but also our spirits as well. We are able to learn from the different events and situations we encounter in our everyday living, and in some cases, others can learn from us.

Keep in mind that we are not only the students, but the teachers as well. We may have to go through those difficult or rough periods in our lives in order to give others the opportunity to help us.

It is my experience from speaking with spirits who committed suicide that they were very remorseful for doing so. On the other side, a spirit understands the bigger picture of why he or she was here to begin with. They come to the realization that whatever problems caused them to take their own lives, eventually they were going to get through them. Ending their lives here on Earth may have erased the physical issues they were going through, only to be replaced by an even bigger one—seeing and feeling the effect of their actions. Once over on the other side, it is not God who will be judging you, as he is ever loving. It is you, judging yourself.

Most of the time, people who commit suicide believe that they are only hurting themselves. On the contrary! Not only are they affecting the lives of the people they know now, but also the people who were to come.

If you would allow me to use another film as an example, think about the Christmas classic *It's a Wonderful Life.* Jimmy Stewart portrays George Bailey, a man who feels boxed in with all of life's problems and is so fed up that he decides maybe it's best just to end it. While getting ready to do so, Clarence, an angel, shows George what life would actually have been like for the town and the people he loves if he had never existed. To cut to the chase, George was shown that everything was completely different in his hometown. People whom he loved were in different situations. The town itself had taken a turn for the worse. Even his brother had passed away from drowning, since George was not there to save him as before. His family, which he had loved so dearly, didn't even exist.

This is what life would have been like for others, if George had never lived.

This film is a great example of how we affect each other in this life.

I will bet you can think of someone right now that you love and cherish. This could be your husband, wife, child, or best friend. You know there wouldn't be anything in the world that you wouldn't do for that person, or they for you. By being with this individual, you have received the greatest gifts of all, those of friendship and love. But what would have happened if these particular people had taken their lives *before* you knew them? How would *your* life be different? Would you, in fact, be the same person that you are now? I doubt it. Everything you do has a *cause and effect* on Earth. It's like throwing a rock in a pond—your choices and what you do in life will have a rippling effect on others.

Suicide is equivalent to skipping preschool, elementary school, and high school, and trying to head straight to college. Once there, you will know you needed more education, more growth.

In Heaven, a spirit will instantly understand the mistake he or she has made by shortening their life, and realize that they still have to go through lessons in Heaven in order to obtain growth. This is acquired with the help of family members who have passed, guides, and also angels who are with them.

Is it any easier to learn these lessons over there?

No, it's actually harder.

In Heaven, those who have committed suicide would not be placed in certain situations that can occur on Earth. Not only that, they bring baggage with them—the effects and emotions their actions caused to those they left behind.

It was a beautiful spring day. Mickey and Claire were excited about the reading they were about to experience. We greeted each other, and I could tell that the energies were good with this couple. They had hopes of hearing from several close relatives, but were open to hearing messages from anybody. I sensed several spirits and could tell that the other side was ready.

I was able to connect with Mickey's father first, a kind gentleman who sent a lot of love to his son and told of wonderful childhood memories that pulled at Mickey's heart.

"Mickey, your father is telling me that he used to pick you up from school from time to time."

"Yes, that's right."

"He is showing me a dime. Something about a dime and how you'd find it in his pocket."

With that, Mickey started to tear up. "We used to play a game. He would always have a dime for me in his pocket, but I'd have to find which one," Mickey said smiling.

"He's showing me an ice cream cone, too."

"That's what I would buy with the money!" Mickey said, laughing.

I continued, "He wants you to know that was a very happy memory for him."

"For me as well, I just haven't thought of it in years," Mickey said.

Mickey's father also told of another time when he and Mickey had gone sledding in the early morning, on the new-fallen snow, long before anyone else had gotten up. It brought back a lot of good memories for Mickey. His father was now going to step aside, but sent Mickey all his love and told him that "Mickey would always be his little boy."

Claire's aunt was next. She was a very responsible person, and cared a great deal for her niece. She thanked Claire for always remembering her. She was especially grateful for the flowers that Claire had just planted in honor of her birthday. They were carnations, her favorite flower.

Though there were different confirmations and messages coming through for both Mickey and Claire, their loved ones wanted to step aside for the next person to come in. The next spirit that came in took them by surprise.

"I have a younger woman here who I feel is not a close relative, yet is connected to you. May I bring her in?" I asked.

"Please do," said Claire, who was still smiling from the message of love from her aunt.

"Okay, the first thing she is showing me is her beautiful long black hair. She said she was known for it."

Claire looked puzzled, yet remained open.

"She is also letting me know that she was at one time part of your family, and that you do know her."

Both Mickey and Claire were concentrating, but still they saw no connection. Everything else had been going great up to this point, so I wasn't about to give up. I felt everyone else had stepped aside to let this spirit come through, so I knew she had something special to convey.

By the way she was coming to me, I could feel that this woman had committed suicide. A soul that has gone through this comes in with what I would refer to as a lower vibration. There is a heaviness felt that I can compare only to how one may feel when in an extremely sad, depressed mood.

"I am now sensing a lot of sorrow from her, and she is telling me that she committed suicide."

While I was saying this, my hand subconsciously shaped itself as a gun and I pointed it at my mouth.

"She shot herself," I said.

Hearing and seeing that jolted the couple and it was enough for them to know exactly what I was talking about.

"Oh my God, that would be Melanie!" Claire cried out. "Melanie took her own life because of her overwhelming sadness, which her family never understood."

The couple grew quiet while this began to unfold.

"She was in a relationship with one of your family members, Claire," I said.

Still shook up, Claire just nodded her head yes.

"Well, I am getting that she and her boyfriend or husband were apart when this happened."

As those words came out of my mouth, Melanie was giving me the feeling that I was going in the wrong direction, about her mate. I silently asked her why, and she answered.

"Oh, I'm sorry, she says it wasn't a boyfriend or husband, but another woman."

The two agreed that it was.

Claire's sister Terry had had a relationship with Melanie. The two had been a close couple and made no attempts to hide their feelings from other family members. Terry's family accepted that she was gay, but Melanie's family had not. They were old school, and felt Melanie's attraction to another woman was a sin.

"Melanie wanted to come in today to give you messages with the hope that you would pass them along, not only to help her, but to help her family as well," I said.

Mickey asked. "What type of messages?"

"She first wants everyone to know that she is extremely sorry for taking her own life. Being on the other side, she not only sees, but also *feels*, all the effects and emotions she has caused by cutting her life short. Because she committed suicide, Melanie had to face what she had done, and come to an understanding it was wrong. She has done this with the help of angels and guides who are with her.

"But the pain she is feeling now is her family's pain. Her mother, along with other family members are, in a way, keeping her from going to the next level due to . . . believe it or not, their prayers."

Puzzled, Claire asked, "Are prayers not helpful?"

I continued, "Yes, prayers are extremely helpful, if they come from the right place. Melanie is telling me her mother keeps praying for God to forgive her for taking her own life and for being gay. Her mother has to come to understand that when someone loves another person, no matter what gender, race, or creed, it is not wrong. For why would God give us the greatest gift in the world, love, and place limits and prejudices on it?

"*He didn't . . . we did.*

"Once her mother realizes that God has forgiven Melanie for taking her own life, this will start the healing process for both. The bond between Melanie and her mother has never been broken. But with her mother continuing to be so negative, not only is she feeling this effect, but Melanie is as well."

At this point, the couple agreed that they would, in fact, relay this message.

"Melanie is grateful to you both for allowing her the time to come and talk with you. She knows this was your time with your own friends and relatives, and thanks you both for your understanding and help."

It never fails to amaze me how the other side works. Claire and Mickey's family in spirit, although anxious to speak to them, stepped aside to let this intense message come through.

A month later, I heard from Claire and Mickey. They told me how they relayed all this to Melanie's family. Melanie's mother not only accepted the information but broke down and wept. Hearing that her daughter was in fact not burning in Hell, but being aided by God, helped the mother to cope. She also did come to understand that in order to help her daughter she first had to forgive Melanie, and also to forgive herself. She had been in torment since the passing of her daughter and now felt that a heaviness had been lifted from her heart. The love she once had for her daughter returned and filled her heart with a joy that had long been missing. She now not only prays positively to Melanie, but talks to her daughter daily as well. She realized she too had lessons to learn, and together they can—even with Melanie on the other side.

The above is an example of someone who knew at the time that he or she was taking their own life. Is the outcome the same for a person who didn't realize what he or she was doing?

No.

If someone was mentally ill, or his or her physical mind took complete control over their logical reasoning, the outcome would not be the same. Others around this individual may have needed to go through this type of loss for their own spiritual growth.

I have also talked with numerous people who had considered taking their own lives, due to the overwhelming grief they had been experiencing from the loss of a loved one. People in this situation feel the only way to *reconnect* with passed loved ones is to join them on the other side.

This is definitely the wrong thing to do!

Though they may reunite with their loved one *physically* on the other side, they will not be at the same level *spiritually*. And again, the spiritual level is what is important. Instead of being together, they would find themselves trying to work out the effect of their actions.

If you know someone who has committed suicide, you should pray for their souls with compassion and understanding. On the other side they have come to realize they did have other choices. Having our love and forgiveness will help their souls continue to grow. Never believe that it is too late to help heal someone.

Even though someone is in Heaven, your love and forgiveness can and will work miracles for him or her.

11

Keeping your personality in heaven

Once people reach the other side, they become aware of what their lives were all about, and what Heaven holds for them?

True.

In acquiring this kind of knowledge, do their souls become completely different from who and what they were here on Earth?

Not a chance!

Our personality is our soul! It is who we are and what we are. It is the personality with whom we become friends or we fall in love with. Though you may have a richer understanding in Heaven, and may be humbled by what knowledge you now have, still, you are who you are.

During a reading, it would be almost impossible for me to determine what spirits I was communicating with if not for their unique personalities. It is what their loved ones here on Earth recognize, their *spirit thumbprint*. The personality is one of the first senses I receive when speaking with someone on the other side. If a person was soft-spoken here on Earth, he or she will be soft-spoken in spirit. If someone was very vocal and had high energy, that is who this person is over there as well.

I was giving a reading for a client named Laura. Things were going well, and several of her relatives had come through and given great messages. In the middle of the session, the spirit of a young and very energetic woman interrupted us. I can sum up a spirit's personality quickly, and this spirit had waited long enough. The young woman was named Shelly, and I will not soon forget her.

"There is a young lady here, and she is telling me that it is her turn now," I explained to Laura. "She has waited long enough."

"Fine," Laura said.

"There must have been an age difference between the two of you since she is laughing at this and keeps referring to herself as 'kid' even though she is not a child."

Shelly and her husband Ben had just moved to Atlanta a year and a half before. She and Laura met and became instant friends. It took no time at all for Laura to introduce Shelly to all of her friends, which made Shelly feel comfortable in her new surroundings.

"While Shelly's husband Ben was the same age as the rest of us, she was about nine to ten years younger," Laura said. "She always got teased about her age."

Laura was very happy to hear from her friend and had hoped that she would.

"Shelly is quite vocal," I told her. "She is the type of person who will say what is on her mind."

Laura agreed.

"She gets what she wants, she's almost bratty," I explained. "If things did not go her way, she was not happy."

"That's our Shelly," Laura exclaimed.

I continued, "She is not a bad person in any way, just has a really strong personality."

Laura confirmed this by telling me that at Shelly's funeral, her mother's eulogy told of Shelly's strong leadership and how she always got what she wanted. She never let anyone get in her way. Though her personality was a little strong sometimes, she was young and still learning.

"Shelly is showing me a cheerleading outfit and is telling me that she was the one to pump up the crowd," I said.

"Shelly was a cheerleader in high school!" Laura confirmed excitedly. "She was definitely one to pump up the crowd."

Moving on, Shelly started to tell me of her passing. I could feel how excited she was to communicate with her friend, and she was not about to stop.

"Shelly passed in a car accident," I said. "It was an accident, not her fault, and she passed quickly."

Laura, amazed, confirmed this.

After the accident, Shelly was rushed to the hospital and right into surgery. Ben waited hour after hour in the lobby, yearning to hear any word about his wife. Eventually word did come, and Ben was able to see Shelly once she had awakened from the procedure. Shelly had a calm, relaxed look, and told Ben that everything was going to be okay. After a few minutes of talking with him, Shelly told Ben she needed to rest and asked him to go home and get her pajamas and glasses. Ben left, and by the time he came back to the hospital, he had a strong sense that Shelly had left him.

This feeling became a reality.

While Ben was gone, Shelly had gone into cardiac arrest and lost oxygen, which left her brain-dead. Ben was devastated, but kept his beloved wife "alive" on machines until the family flew in to say their goodbyes.

This is an example of how some souls will wait for their loved ones to leave before they pass over. They know when it is time and want to spare them that pain.

The reading continued.

"Shelly is now telling me that although she did not pass immediately, she did observe her body at the accident and—her words, not mine. It was a mess!" I said. "She is also saying she was not at all happy about the way people saw her at the end. She did not look like herself and is laughing about that."

Laura smiled and nodded as well. "The one thing you could always say about Shelly," Laura exclaimed, "is she always looked great. Her face was completely swollen from all the medication, and they had to put a lot of makeup on her face," Laura continued. "Shelly was someone who never had to wear much makeup. Ben even made a remark that Shelly would have been mad if she knew what she looked like."

Laura was relieved Shelly was laughing, since they were all a little worried about how she would feel about the way she had looked.

"Shelly is telling me you ought to see how she dresses now and the best part is, it doesn't cost her a dime for the clothes!"

"She always dressed so nice." Laura said laughingly. "I would call her the 'J. Crew Girl' because Shelly always looked as if she belonged on the cover of a magazine. I understand the 'not costing a dime' thing too," Laura said. "Shelly loved to shop at Anne Taylor's. It was a bit expensive for her with an average salary, but she loved to dress nice. Shelly would talk about how she wanted to make a lot of money so she could buy all the clothes she wanted."

Laura was amazed that Shelly was coming through just as she had in life, talking about what was important to her.

"Now I can see how women can chat on the phone for hours," I said, jokingly.

"Shelly is mentioning to me how much she likes water, she is still with water, and she says she has earned it!"

Laura excitedly told me, "Yes, that is right, Ben and Shelly had bought a house by a lake. That is where Shelly's ashes are scattered." Laura further explained, "When they first purchased the house, they found it had been horribly decorated. They didn't have a ton of money, so Shelly shopped all the outlet malls and found some outrageous deals. After her passing, Ben started to get all the furniture Shelly had ordered. Shelly wanted a sailboat theme, so, for her, he kept it."

"You can see, by her comments, Shelly is enjoying the furniture," I said.

Shelly's energy level was still high and she had more to tell Laura. The best was yet to come.

"Shelly is telling me about the book you borrowed," I said. "It's okay for your husband to keep it."

Laura smiled and explained, still amazed with what was transpiring. "We used to swap books all the time. One of the last books we borrowed was *Pillars of the Earth*, which was for my husband, Matt. Shelly had asked about the book a month before she had passed, and I told her I would get after Matt about it."

Laura said it could take Matt forever to finish a book, because he tended to read four or five of them at a time.

"Every weekend I would apologize to Shelly because Matt was still reading it."

I laughed and said, "Shelly is saying not to worry about it, she has her own copy now."

Laura shook her head and smiled.

"Shelly is also telling me that she was standing right beside you as you were holding a picture of her today," I said.

"Oh my gosh," Laura exclaimed. She had asked Shelly to come through and say something about the picture so as to have a confirmation. Matt had taken a picture of her and Shelly on the back of their boat Memorial Day weekend, two weekends prior to her death.

"I'm so excited," Laura said. "I got the film developed the day after she passed. I asked Shelly (thinking that I was completely crazy) to put a smudge or something in the picture. When I got the picture back there was something quite remarkable on it. On the picture, across Shelly's legs, was a rainbow and what appeared to be a light sun smear over her head. It was the only picture that Shelly was in and the last one of her alive. It was the only picture like that!"

Seeing this photo made Laura realize that you can request signs from loved ones, but you have to be ready to notice them.

"Shelly wants you to know she is a ghost now," I exclaimed. "Not really, she's just teasing you. She is telling me that she is really an angel and she has her wings!" Shelly was laughing as she was telling me this.

Laura said Shelly would always say, "Hey girl," and this coming through and the way it was emphasized in the reading made her laugh out loud.

"I know what 'angel' she is talking about, too!" Laura said. "I went to get a frame for the picture of Shelly and myself, and was looking for one with the word 'friends' on it. I found what I thought was the perfect one, and on it was written, 'ANGELS, sweet protectors.'"

Laura was overjoyed with her friend's messages.

"Shelly is saying she waited to be the last to come in, so that the 'old folks' could be first."

"That was Shelly," Laura said with a smile.

Now, I have made a promise to the other side to reveal everything they give me during a reading, but in my conversation with Shelly she threw me for a loop! I was bringing Laura all of these wonderful confirmations of love when all of a sudden I had a spirit do something I had never seen before.

Shelly *flashed* me!

Believe me, I was shocked and very surprised by this. Here I am conveying warm and thoughtful messages from Shelly, and she flashes her breasts at me! I started thinking—why in the world would she do that? Do I tell Laura about this? Is Shelly just being her old self and pulling a trick on me? Keep in mind that all of this is going on while I am still telling Laura what Shelly had previously said. I am usually one step ahead of the conversation—I am literally between two conversations.

My belief is that spirits do not show or tell me things unless these mean something—in this case, it better had!

"Laura, I have to tell you something, and I hope it connects because I am embarrassed to tell you," I said.

Laura said, "What is it?"

"Well," I continued, "Shelly just exposed her breasts to me. I don't know why, but I really hope this means something to you."

I waited for her response, and you know what? It didn't mean a thing to Laura!

Now, at this point, my face turned beet red. We both started to laugh (thank God) but Shelly kept exposing her breasts to me and was laughing right along.

"Laura, are you sure?" I inquired. "She keeps flashing me, it must mean something!" I continued. "Was she known to do this? Was she especially proud of her breasts?" I was hanging on by a thread here.

Though still laughing, Laura could make no connection.

"Okay, just keep it in mind, because she says that it will come to you."

Thank God, it did!

Laura, Matt, Shelly, and Ben had plans to go to New Orleans for Mardi Gras. Laura remembered talking with Shelly about how people riding floats in the parade would toss bead necklaces to women who would lift up their shirts. Though they wanted some of the necklaces, the two were unsure if they had enough nerve to do this. Laura now understood that Shelly was telling her to go ahead, go on the trip and have fun! Shelly would be there too. Laura said it was just like Shelly's personality to tell us to go ahead on that trip in that fashion.

I was so glad Laura (and I) finally understood what Shelly was telling her to do. What an eccentric way to do it, but that was—and is—Shelly.

12

Dogs go to heaven

As any pet owners will tell you, their pet is part of the family. What makes us love animals so much? Is it the way they look? Is it that they're good company? Yes, to all of the above, but we also love their personalities. If you own a pet, you know exactly what I am talking about.

Someone who owns several pets could tell you, in detail, the exact character traits of each one. Where do their personalities come from? Well, just as we discussed—their souls. Yes, animals have souls, too!

And where do souls go? To Heaven.

People wonder if it is possible for me to speak with their pets on the other side. The answer is, at times, yes. Loved ones on the other side may show or tell me during a reading that a particular pet is with them, showing they are safe and in good hands. The loved ones themselves will relay this message. At times though, I will actually receive a message from the pet itself. No, the pet will not start *talking* to me as if it had a voice. What they will do is use clairvoyance or clairaudience, or clairsentience, which is using images, sounds, or feelings to relay a message.

At times, their messages can be up for interpretation.

One Saturday, Kathy and I went to Orlando, Florida, to do several seminars. As usual, I opened with a small meditation for the group, and was ready to begin with the readings. Several spirits came through, and I relayed messages to their family and friends who were in the audience. It was going quite well, with several humorous messages coming in as well as many touching stories filling the hours. I sipped my water to quench my thirst and asked if anyone had any questions.

A young woman raised her hand and asked, "Can you contact dogs that have passed away? I had one, and would really like to know if he's okay."

Well, again, just like with any reading, it's not up to me, it's up to the other side, but I told her that I would be willing to give it a try.

I started to open myself up, to see if I would connect with the energy of her dog. Again, when doing this, I do not know if the pet itself is going to come in, or if a loved one will be bringing it in. This time, it was going to be the dog.

I started to see the little guy running around, and tried my best to get him to keep still. Just like with any human, they are who they are, and this one was a rascal.

"Was your dog small, and ran around constantly? Because the one that is here sure is!"

The crowd laughed, and she responded, "He sure was and did. His name is Cubby!"

"Well, Cubby is still running around!" I said jokingly. "I'm trying to get him to stop for a moment!"

"Oh good!" she replied.

"Well, I can tell you Cubby is very happy to be here, and is showing me that you still have his food, is this true?"

"Yes, I haven't been able to throw it away yet."

"Okay," I said, "let me see what else I can get. Did you just remove his name tag off his collar? He is showing me you taking it off," I said.

"Yes, I wanted to keep it with me as a remembrance," she said.

I replied. "Well, he seems happy that you did this."

Everyone in the room listened on.

"Did Cubby used to scratch and chew furniture?"

Puzzled, the woman said, "No."

I said, "He's showing me furniture, and it is very scratched and chewed."

"Let me think for a moment—no, I don't believe he did," she replied.

I asked Cubby to give me more.

"Believe it or not, he's not letting this go. He must have scratched furniture, he keeps showing me a table leg with marks on it."

"Oh I know, I'll bet he's talking about the back door! He would always scratch at the door to be let out, and this made marks on it."

As much as I would have liked to say yes, I knew that wasn't what Cubby was showing me.

"I'm going to say no to that. He keeps showing me a table leg, not a door, so I'm going to stick with what I am seeing. This is a challenge now, and we're going to get this," I said, smiling.

There was silence in the room. Everyone was hanging on to every word, because they wanted the puzzle solved, too.

"Okay, let me try this again . . . this is what I am seeing. He is showing me a table, but more than that, a leg on the table, and he is chewing it."

"No, he never did that," she said.

The room was so quiet you could hear a pin drop.

"Yes, he did," I said. "He chewed the leg off!"

She was shaking her head no, so I finally blurted out, "Did he chew his *own* leg off?"

Her eyes widened, and she shouted out, "Yes! He did chew his own leg completely off!"

And with that, the whole audience gasped.

While this young lady was trying to cage train Cubby, one day she had left him in the large cage with a blanket because she was going to work. The blanket had some quilting on it, and the seams were sewn with invisible thread, much like nylon fishing line. Cubby, walking around in the cage, tangled his leg with a loose piece of thread. Being caught, and becoming nervous, he started to turn around and around in the cage, causing the thread to become tighter and tighter, until it cut off the circulation to his foot. Like most animals, he panicked, tried to get free, and started to chew at his leg. He couldn't feel his foot, so he didn't realize what he was doing. Luckily, this injury was not fatal, and Cubby spent many happy years with her.

This was the perfect bit of information to confirm to the owner that her dog was there, communicating with us.

Pets are an important part of so many people's lives, because they give us unconditional love. Once again, love never dies, nor do they. *It wouldn't be Heaven without them now, would it?*

Part IV

❧

Insights

In the following section, I would like to share with you some of the things that I have learned from speaking with those on the other side.

13

Questions from earth, answers from above

First, I, too, am just as anxious to know exactly what Heaven is like and what we have waiting for us once we pass. But you also should know, spirits can only convey things that can be perceived by our human mind. Heaven is beyond anything we can imagine. It would be the same as if we were viewing a color television show on a black-and-white TV. Though the show (Heaven) is in color, the black-and-white TV (our human minds) could never portray its true magnificence. Spirits tell me there are no words that could ever come close to describing what it is really like.

The Questions

Why are we here?

We are born of this physical body, but we are first and foremost spirit. We come into this life to be placed in situations that will enhance our spiritual growth. It is up to us whether or not we grow from these experiences. All of the feelings and emotions that are brought forth through our actions and reactions in any situation become part of us and contribute to our soul's growth. By enriching our souls with love, we become closer to God.

Is there a God?

Yes, but for us to fully understand who or what God is, is again beyond our human comprehension. Spirits tell me God is a part of every living thing, and every living thing is a part of God. He and his love are the light that illuminates Heaven. The sun is but a faint candle in comparison. God is ever forgiving, ever knowing, and ever loving. God is always present. God is life. God is!

In Heaven, you exist in a greater awareness and understanding of God, but always know that we do not have to be on the other side to see or experience God. He and his love surround us, always. Look into the eyes of a child when he sees the presents under the Christmas tree on Christmas morning, the face of a bride as she sees her husband pronounce his love, or the gleaming face of a parent with his or her newborn child. Look also inside your own heart.

When you do kind things for others, God is there, with you and in you. These are all reflections of God.

Is there a Heaven?

Heaven is a real place. It is tangible, and it goes beyond what we know as three dimensional. It is not only a place you see, but also a place that you feel.

Most of us are told that if you are good, you will go to Heaven, and if you are bad, you will go to Hell. Well, that leaves room for a lot of gray area! What is good, and what is bad?

Is being rich and donating a lot of money to charity or a church, not because it comes from the heart, but because it will help you with a tax break, being good?

Is not donating money to a charity or a church because you cannot afford to, but wish that you could, being bad?

It's not necessarily your physical actions that count, but where your heart is that determines *good* or *bad*. This, and this alone, will determine where you are, once on the other side.

There are different levels on the other side. Try not to think of these in physical terms, but in an emotional or spiritual sense. There, one will go to the level in which they are spiritually equal with others, depending on their deeds in life and their spiritual growth on Earth.

Like souls are with like souls.

This is not to say that we are separated from our family and friends who may not be on the same level. Quite the contrary. We may be in different grades, but all exist with each other.

In Heaven, there are land, flowers, trees, and animals. Nature is present and flourishing over there. The colors in Heaven are more vibrant than we can imagine. Not only do we see nature's beauty, but actually *feel* it as well. Take a flower, for instance. On Earth, we are able to look at a flower, touch it, and smell its scent. In Heaven, we also are able to connect with its energy. We are able to connect with the energy of all living things.

People can and do live in houses there. The houses we have depend on us. More than likely, the first house we will go to will probably be one from our past, something in which we are comfortable. This may make the transition easier. I remember talking to a man on the other side who was a builder. He told his wife here on Earth that he was building their dream home. He described it to me as Victorian style, with a porch that surrounded the house. He said they would have the small creek they always wanted, that it ran under a bridge near the house. His wife couldn't believe it because I had described the house they always wished for, but couldn't afford. In Heaven, you are able to have what you have earned here on Earth.

You might have heard Heaven is always sunny and warm—don't believe it! I have talked to many spirits who have told me it can be cloudy, snowy, rainy—all the seasons you might enjoy here.

Believe it or not, they even have food! Though it is not necessary to eat on the other side, it is really just for pleasure. Bakers and chefs over there have to keep busy, too!

I once made a connection to a spirit who told me she was about to go to a friend's house to have a barbecue. Why should that sound strange to us? Why wouldn't we have the same pleasures we enjoyed here?

They also celebrate holidays over there. My own mother has told me of the many times the family has gotten together for holidays and a gathering around the table. It would have to be a big table because she has twelve siblings. Keep in mind it is love that surrounds the fun-filled gatherings we have here on Earth, as well as in Heaven. The great thing about those on the other side is that not only do they celebrate with those who have crossed over, but also continue to celebrate with us here on Earth. It truly is the best of both worlds. It is a real environment, with real people, living life.

Many envision Heaven being somewhere far off, well beyond our Universe. It is quite the opposite. The Earth, and this Universe, are all a part of Heaven.

Is Earth Hell?

You may have heard the statement, or even used it yourself, "If there is a Heaven, then Earth must be Hell."

Can you imagine what God thinks when hearing this?

God has given us so many beautiful and wondrous things to enjoy on Earth. Every second on this Earth is a gift, a miracle. It is only those not appreciative of it who call it a Hell. Anything we feel is wrong with this Earth has not been caused by God, but by us. The important thing is to learn and grow from any negative events that we may experience.

Kathy has a great saying: "If you think you have a problem, just wait five minutes, look around, and you will see someone worse off than yourself. Then your problem doesn't seem so bad." I love that saying because it is so true. We have to put things in perspective. Yes, there can be a lot of challenges here, to say the least, but so what! Don't you usually get past them? And when you do, don't you feel as if you have grown from them? Guess what, that's what we're here for in the first place—to love, learn, and then go home!

Is there a Hell?

Yes, but on the other side it is the state of existing at a lower level, a lower state of being.

Does God put you there?

No, you put yourself there.

On the other side, you see and feel the effect you had on every single person you encountered on Earth. Those who led a life that caused harm, pain, or was filled with hatred toward others will encounter all this negativity. Again, it becomes a part of them. God does forgive, as he is ever loving and never vengeful.

I want to repeat that. *God is never vengeful.*

But you are the one who will have to forgive yourself. On the other side, that is the hardest thing to do. There, you see all of the possibilities of what could have been, but things that you yourself denied. We have to sort through our own actions and feel how they have affected others. We are given counseling and advice from those on higher levels, but we have free will to accept any and all help, or not.

So anyone who is in the state of "Hell" is there forever?

"Forever" is a term we use time and again, but there is no such thing as time on the other side. Once individual souls see, understand, and come to terms with how they have lived, they have the opportunity to raise themselves up to be closer with God. They can do that by coming back and living life again on Earth or helping souls from over there who are on the same path as they were.

It's much like Charles Dickens' *The Christmas Carol.* Marley came back to help Scrooge realize all the mistakes and missed opportunities that he had while he was living. God was not punishing Marley. Marley was punishing himself after having lived such a selfish and lonely life.

God is gracious enough to let us lead our own lives, and though we receive help from spirits every day, it is up to us to listen.

Do we have bodies in Heaven?

There are two different bodies that we have on this Earth, one physical, the other spiritual. On Earth, our spiritual body, or soul, is shelled by our physical body. It is within this body that we experience physical pain or pleasure on this Earth. In Heaven, it's the opposite. It is your spiritual body that surrounds your physical body.

When you are met by your loved ones on the other side, any signs of aging, disease, or illness will not exist with them, since these things do not exist in Heaven. If you knew someone who had passed when elderly—let's say a grandparent—he or she could come to you as younger. It will be as if they were in the prime of their life. A child who passes will continue to grow, not only spiritually, but physically, though his or her physical growth would not necessarily occur in the same time frame as on Earth.

No matter what changes a person might have had on the other side, you will know instantly who they are. You will recognize their spiritual essence. This is also seen on the other side. Your spiritual appearance is the core of who you are in Heaven. Your spiritual body also can have its aches and pains, but they are very different.

An example of this is when your heart aches for a loved one. It's not actually your heart that is aching, but your soul. See the difference?

Another example: When you look at yourself in a photograph or a mirror, do you feel your age? Some of you will feel younger than your physical age, and some of you will feel older. Again, I'm not talking about how your physical body feels, but how you feel inside yourself. You can also feel old about some things and young about others. Your spirit is made from the many experiences you have had, and it is from these experiences that your soul ages.

What happens when we die?

The soul knows when it is time to exit the body. If a person passes after a long illness and suffering, his or her soul may be in and out of the body, preparing itself for the transition. Many spirits I have spoken with who were in a coma before passing were able to stand next to their body and watch, listen, and feel their loved ones who were standing beside them. If you were ever in a situation such as this, never doubt that your loved ones heard your prayers. They did.

I have also been told that shedding the body, especially one that has been suffering through a long and lingering illness, is like shedding an old, heavy overcoat. Such spirits whom I have communicated with are extremely happy to be rid of it.

If someone passes quickly, as in a car accident, they might at first be a little disoriented and confused about what has happened to them. Who wouldn't be? Imagine driving along one minute, and the next, you're in Heaven! That could be jolting, to say the least. More often than not, spirits in this situation tell me they actually viewed the accident from out of their bodies, and while doing so, felt no pain. Were their lives cut short? Not likely. Again, what might seem like accidents to us are not. We come here to learn lessons, as well as to teach others; some souls can do this in the span of a normal lifetime, others can do it more quickly.

When a soul passes over, they never go through the transition by themselves. Though you may have known someone in your life who you thought might have been alone when he or she made the transition to the other side, I can promise you, they were not. Every one of us has loved ones, guides, and angels who will help us with our transition. They are there to answer any and all questions we might have at the time.

And keep in mind; though we tend to feel the passing of a loved one as someone leaving, on the other side it is the opposite because our relatives and friends in spirit see it is a happy arrival.

Along the same lines, some people have told me how guilty they felt that they had left an ill family member for just a moment, and by the time they came back the person had passed away.

Let me tell you, that is not due to bad timing or by accident. Many times spirits will tell me that they waited for their loved one to leave the room before they passed on. Spirits will sometimes say humorously that they thought their loved ones would never leave!

So if this has, or should ever happen to you, never feel guilty about it. A soul knows when it is time to go home.

So now you have been greeted by loved ones, guides, and angels. What's next?

After your *reunion* on the other side, you have what you would call a *life review* or your *test score*. I know you've heard of people saying they have seen their life flash before their eyes. Well it is true. God will show you every moment of your life as you reflect on your soul's growth. But the one thing you may or may not know about your review is that you not only see your whole life, but *feel* your whole life as well. This would include how you made other people feel. As the golden rule says, "Do unto others as you would have them do unto you." Truer words were never written. Here's an example of what this is like.

Let's say that one day I was in a bad mood. I went into a store, already angry, and yelled at the clerk. I took my angry feelings and placed them on him. This clerk, now being in a bad mood, yells at a fellow employee, and this employee gets angry at another customer. On the other side, I not only feel how I made the employee feel, but I feel the whole chain reaction, the one that I originally caused. As stated before, your feelings and those you cause are your core essence in Heaven, and you do not want negative energies to be a part of your soul.

Keep in mind that the opposite holds true as well. You are in a great mood, you go into a store and compliment the clerk. He or she may have been having a bad day, but your comments have put them in a good mood, which in turn they pass on to someone else. On the other side, this whole positive chain reaction becomes a part of you as well.

During your review, you will make a connection with your loved ones who are still here in this world. You will see and feel how others react to your passing and your life. You will receive their feeling toward you—good or bad. During this time, you will comfort your loved ones and send positive and loving energy their way.

I know that most of you have sensed your loved ones when attending their funeral. This is because you *actually* did feel them. This is their way of connecting with you. It is truly a shame that a lot of people just pass this off as imagination. Those of you who do not, know how fortunate you are.

Are spirits sad for us?

I have been asked many times if those who have passed over are sad for those they left behind, having to go through such grief. They are not necessarily sad, but *sympathetic* for their loved ones. They now have a greater understanding of what life is really about. They see the bigger picture and know they are still with their loved ones here on Earth.

It is as if you were with a child who had lost his or her favorite toy. At that moment, the child is devastated, and the world seems to come to an end. Even though you know what this toy meant for the child, as an adult you understand he or she will get through their sadness. You will comfort the child and do what you can to help.

From spirits' viewpoints, we are the children, they are the adults, and will comfort us any way they are able to.

What do spirits do once on the other side?

Well, let me tell you, if you imagine all the souls over there laying on clouds all day, playing harps, think again.

Our loved ones will *do things* in Heaven. Call them jobs if you want to, but they don't think of it in that way. Someone who loved children here might choose to help children that have passed over. Those who enjoyed teaching will do so on the other side, as spiritual growth and learning does continues there. Pet lovers may welcome newcomers to the other side and find homes for these recently arrived animal spirits. There are as many tasks over there as our human minds can imagine, even more so.

There, you will not only do things for each other, you may want to also help those on Earth. Spirits who had a certain profession or expertise, such as a doctor, teacher, artist, or singer, just to name a few, will help those who have the same talent or ability here. They will assist by guiding them in using their God-given gifts to the best of their abilities. We are all blessed with the help of spirit, every day.

Do they have fun on the other side?

If you lead a good life, imagine being in perfect heath, having anything you want, doing anything you want, and being anywhere you want. Sounds like Heaven, right?

Well, it is!

As we have now established, Heaven is a solid place where you are able to reap all of its many blessings. Anything that brought you joy here will continue to do so there.

Our loved ones will have gatherings over there with family and friends. During these gatherings they reflect on the joys of being in God's presence and bask in all of the glory. Any activities you can imagine—and some you would never even dream of—are enjoyed over there, from going to concerts to gardening, sports, hiking, boating, swimming, skiing—the list is endless!

You never give up the passions you had here, but there you can live them.

A woman came to me once who wanted to connect to her grandmother who had passed from cancer. In her younger days, her grandmother had been a dancer for the Ziegfield Follies. She used to tell stories of how, in her youth, she was considered a "quite a looker" and how she so enjoyed dancing and performing for people. By the time her daughter, and certainly her granddaughter, had come along, her performing days were very much in her past, only a sweet memory during tea on a rainy afternoon. Her grandmother did, in fact, come through. She wanted her granddaughter to know that she was young again, back on stage, and doing what came naturally to her—bringing joy to those on the other side with her gift of dancing.

Is there such a thing as reincarnation?

Many people ask me if we have more than one life. The answer is yes.

What is the purpose of life? To enhance our souls and to help others do the same. How do we do this? By learning, or having others learn, from situations that we encounter here on Earth.

In thinking of life as a school, in each grade we are taught lessons to increase our knowledge, to become as smart as we can be. Once we finish a grade, we take that knowledge with us to the next level. We couldn't possibly learn second grade lessons until we learned the basics of first grade. Once all the grades are completed, we graduate. This is why we reincarnate, to learn and to teach different spiritual lessons with each life, so that we may graduate to God.

If you think about it, why is reincarnation so hard to accept? You believe the soul entered your body in this lifetime. Why would it be so difficult to believe that it can do that more than once?

Again, God is ever loving and understanding. Why would he just give one chance per soul? How many times do we come back? That is up to us. It depends on what lessons we choose to learn, and how long and how many lifetimes it takes us to learn them.

What are the differences between guardian angels and spirit guides?

While we go through our journey on Earth, we have a main guide who has helped us every step of the way through our life. This is what is referred to as a "spirit guide."

This guide's presence is not known to most people while on Earth, but is with us nevertheless. Many times, people will mistakenly consider these guides as guardian angels—they are not. Spirit guides are souls that have lived on this Earth before. You may have known them in a past life, or not. A spirit guide will help you with the path you have chosen to take in this life, and with the lessons you need to learn. You might even want to consider the guide a *tutor*. You certainly can have more than one guide at a time, depending on what situations you are encountering in your life, but you will have one main guide throughout your entire life. Just as we all have a specialty here, guides have strengths they use to help us in whatever areas we desire. Patience, love, and understanding are just a few of the lessons with which our guides will help us.

Angels guide us also. Guardian angels are beings that have never lived a life on Earth. These holy beings will also help direct us, and be our guides at the times when they are needed. You can call angels the *go-betweens* from humans to God. Don't get me wrong, God is with each and every one of us, always, since we are a part of God. Angels are a race unto themselves. In some ways they are physically different from us, yet have some human characteristics. Their love for God is reflected in their service to us. They protect us, guide us, and comfort us.

Angels and Spirit Guides are just *one more gift* God has given us here on our journey.

What are soul mates?

You hear the term "soul mates" used a lot, but what does it really mean? Is this the person you will marry? Can you have more than one soul mate?

A soul mate is someone with whom you share more than a friendship. It is someone with whom you have a connection or a bond that is like no other. You can have more than one soul mate, but each one will have its own unique qualities.

My sister Kathy and I are soul mates. Unlike other brothers and sisters that we know, Kathy and I have always been close. It is hard to describe in words the bond soul mates have, but you know it when it is there. You are a part of each other. You can tell each other everything, but more than likely you don't have to, because each one already knows the other's truths. There would never be a moment where you would not do anything for the other, nor even have to ask. Soul mates find each other to help one another, or perhaps to help others. They share a bond that can stand the test of time.

Though Kathy and I have the same interests and tastes (most of the time), one can in some ways be completely the opposite of a soul mate. It is not the physical world that bonds you together, but the connection of your souls.

A soul mate can enter your life at any stage. He or she will come to you when the time is right.

What is the difference between religion and spirituality?

There are many religions in the world, and almost all have the same core of truth. It is our human differences that cause variations of that truth.

Spirituality is the core.

It is the pure understanding of God and the universal knowledge of life and the existence of an afterlife. It is a compilation that goes with any religion, any belief. Spirituality should enhance one's faith, not hinder it.

Part V

❧

Never say goodbye

I want to allay any misconceptions or guilt you may have with continuing, or ending, your relationship with your loved ones in Spirit.

14

Not having to let go

I have read in books, or heard others say, that after awhile, you have to *let go* of your loved ones after their passing.

This is absolutely ridiculous.

Heaven is not some far-off place a spirit will go to after hanging around here for awhile, making sure "you're okay."

The fact of the matter is, once a person passes, guess what, they are already in Heaven!

Yes, they are able to relish all that Heaven has and is, but can still *continue* to share in your life here, so as far as keeping them from going to Heaven, you're not.

Let's put it into perspective. Let's say you are a parent, and if given a choice, you have the option of living in paradise *or* being with your child.

Which would you choose?

I will bet your answer is being with your child. Of course it is. And why?

Because no matter what paradise may have to offer, nothing could bring you greater joy and happiness than being with your child. (This certainly also applies to being with a husband, wife, mother, father—anyone you love.)

101

In Heaven, you don't have to make a choice; you get the best of both worlds; enjoying life on the other side and continuing to be a part of your family and friends' life here.

❧

A young lady named Linda had been suffering with the loss of her husband Fred, and came to see me. After his death, Linda read many books about the hereafter and had faith that Fred's life did in fact, continue in Heaven. But Linda felt guilty that her love was keeping him from moving on.

"Linda, your husband is standing right next to me, and I can tell you he has a lot he wants to say."

Linda was very happy to hear this.

I could feel this man had a great deal of love for his wife; it was very tangible.

"Was Fred Irish?" I asked.

"No," she stated.

"Hmmm . . . okay, are you planning a trip to Ireland?"

"Not that I know of," Linda said, giggling.

I smiled. "He's not letting this go; let me work with this for a minute."

I could tell this was important to Fred. He kept showing me a shamrock, and to me that means the person is Irish or is planning a trip to Ireland. I could also tell he was stubborn and wasn't going to let this go. He was enjoying making me work for the information.

"I can tell Fred is the kind of person who likes to make people work for the answer," I said with a smile.

"Oh that's him," Linda said, smiling back.

I continued, "Now he's talking about cooking. These two things go together, they are connected. He says something about the stew, and you should not try it again."

With that, Linda chuckled out loud.

"Irish stew!" she exclaimed. "For our first dinner party, I attempted to make Irish stew, and it was a complete disaster."

"He's telling me that cooking isn't your strong suit, but he loved when you tried," I said.

Linda eyes began to well up with tears of happiness.

Fred had a great sense of humor, and the more the reading went on, the stronger and better communicator he became. I felt the bond between these two was a strong one.

"He's showing me a beach, and saying not a populated one, but a spot where the two of you could be by yourselves."

"Oh yes," she said, "we had a private spot on a beach that was very isolated."

"He tells me you want to go there again, but it is too painful?"

Linda explained that it was their "little bit of Heaven on Earth," and it was just too hard to go there alone.

I replied, "You're not alone, he's telling me to tell you! Don't think of it like that. You know he's always with you, and it would actually do you some good to go," he says.

Fred was stern on this point; he knew this trip would help Linda to heal and still connect with their love and the great memories.

"He is now conveying to me that he wants to talk about the books you have been reading, the spiritual ones."

Linda replied, "Yes, go on."

"Fred is saying he wants to clear up something that you've read."

Linda sat silent in anticipation

"You were reading a book that stated that by your continuing to talk with him, you are keeping him with you and not allowing him to move on."

Linda broke down and started to cry.

"Yes," she said. "I read that our loved ones will stay around with us just for a little while, and then want to move on."

"Fred is telling me to ask you, 'Linda, where would I want to go?!' You were his life here, and you will continue to be it there. He's not going anywhere! He doesn't care what those books are telling you!"

Linda continued to cry, but now with relief and happiness.

Fred wanted me to give her the next statement loud and clear.

"Fred said, 'Linda, understand this . . . *you are part of my Heaven.*'" With that, I started to tear up as well.

After the reading, Linda was very grateful for Fred giving her such a message. She was very concerned that her love for him would keep him from doing the things he needed to do. With his message, she now understood that giving out love is never wrong, for those here and for those in Heaven.

∾

The love bonds we share with others never die, even with passing over. Yes, they do want you to let go of any grief you may have for them and yourself, but not to permanently let go or to stop your love and relationship you have for them.

Again, the wonderful feelings you have toward those on the other side actually help them, becoming a part of their soul. By having love for someone on the other side and knowing that they are still with you, you are making them happier than you could possibly ever realize.

It doesn't matter if it's been three months after a passing or thirty years, your loved ones will always be with you.

15

$\mathscr{T}$he "moving on" misconception

Some of you may be asking, what if you lost your wife or husband, and you want to, or have, remarried. Was it, or is it, okay to *move on*?

The answer is definitely, positively, yes.

As I explained in the previous section, a passed mate will always continue to be a part of your life, that is, as long as you want or need them to be. Never feel they may be upset or angry with you for finding someone else, because love has no limitations.

Alice sat in front of me, waiting for me to make my first connection for her. She was a woman in her fifties, and there were a few issues she wanted to try to resolve by contacting her husband on the other side.

"I have to tell you Alice, your husband is not even giving me a chance to really open up. He's telling me he's ready now!" I said.

"That is definitely him!" Alice replied. "He never was one to wait!"

We both started laughing.

"I'm feeling he had what I call a natural passing, meaning he was not in any type of accident."

"That is correct," said Alice.

I sat for a moment in silence as Alice's husband started giving me the feeling of his passing.

"I now feel a pressure in my brain, and I'm also seeing dots in front of my eyes. Did your husband pass because of some type of brain tumor?"

"Yes. It was cancer of the brain," Alice said.

"Okay, I'm telling him he can stop letting me feel that now, we got the point."

"He always had one to make," she said.

Again, we both laughed.

"I'm hearing something like 'Kel, Kelly.' "

Alice jumped in excitedly, "His name is Kelsey!"

"Okay, close enough," I said, smiling. "He's also showing me he's bald!"

"I would say that he lost his hair during his illness, but he never had much to begin with," Alice said.

"He still doesn't . . . even in Heaven," I replied. "He wants to thank you so much for all you did during his illness . . . it really meant everything to him."

"There's was nothing I would not do for him, he knows that," Alice said tearfully.

"You bet he does," I said. "There's also an eight associated with his passing."

"It was eight years ago this April," Alice said.

The reading continued with other confirmations of life events they had both shared, but when Kelsey started to talk about the present, Alice became a little on edge.

"Kelsey wants you to know how happy he is for you now."

Alice asked, "He is?"

"I have no idea why he's so happy, but I can tell you he is . . . it has something to do with an event that has just taken place. Let me ask."

I took a moment to let Kelsey answer me.

"He's showing me a wedding cake. Someone just got married."

Alice actually started to tremble a little.

"Well, yes," she said.

"Wait a minute, he keeps pointing to you . . . are you the one who just got married?" I asked with a smile.

"Yes, yes," she replied again.

"Well, I have to tell you something I think you need to hear. Kelsey is telling me you might think he is upset you fell in love with someone else. That is 'ludicrous' he is saying . . . his words, not mine. He couldn't be any happier for you!"

Alice gave a sigh of relief.

"I know he knew how much I loved him, and I still do. But I did fall in love, and married someone else, and have been worried about what his thoughts were about my remarrying."

"See, he answered your question before you even asked it," I said.

"He sure did!" Alice replied.

"You may not believe this, but he is telling me he was standing right next to you when you got married again."

"That's so amazing, your saying this," Alice replied excitedly, "because I thought I actually felt him beside me while I was saying my vows. I thought it was my imagination!"

"Well, it wasn't!" I said, laughing.

"In fact, Kelsey is giving me a thumbs up about your new husband. He's telling me, not only does he approve of him, but also he likes his style of cars. What does that mean?" I asked.

Alice started laughing. "My new husband Tad just bought us a new Mercedes. I told him we didn't need anything so expensive, but he felt I would be safer driving it."

"Kelsey agrees with him," I said. "Something to do with the way you drive or something . . . but I'm not going there," I said.

"Some things never change," Alice replied, shaking her head.

∾

Love knows no boundaries, nor does it have limits.

It's certainly all right to find new love after losing another, but again, it's up to you. Never prevent yourself from experiencing love or other wonderful life adventures because of the guilt you may feel about those on the other side.

Your happiness is truly *their* happiness.

16

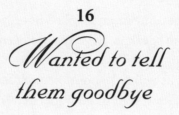

Wanted to tell them goodbye

Another concern I run across with people is when they never had the chance to say "goodbye" to someone who has passed. For whatever reason, they were not present when a loved one went over to the other side and feel as though they never will have a chance for closure.

Let me ask you a question. If you believe your loved ones are continually watching over you, helping and guiding you, why would you want or need to say "goodbye" to them anyway?

The word "goodbye" really makes it sound as if the connection to a loved one is over, that is, until you are reunited with them in Heaven. I can tell you, you are setting yourself up for sadness and depression by placing a distance between you and those who have passed.

A woman named Beverly came to see me one day. She had never been to a medium before, but had a pain in her heart that ran deep. She said she would try anything for some closure. I had her relax and breathe deep. I had to urge her twice to calm down because I could feel she was extremely nervous.

A female presence came in, and I asked Beverly if it was her mother whom she wanted to speak to. Beverly's eyes were filled with tears as she answered yes.

"Sometimes spirits will talk about themselves, or you, but usually both," I said. "Right now, your mom wants to talk about you."

"Okay," Beverly said.

"You must be educated because she places books all around you," I said.

"Yes, I did go to college," Beverly said.

"Though you have a degree, it is not what you do for a living. Does this make sense?"

"Perfect sense."

"I feel such pride from your mother, and she keeps saying 'old people,' so this must be what you do," I said.

"That is is my occupation, I help take care of the elderly," Beverly replied.

"Well, she wants you to know that you're doing an excellent job, and help a lot of people!" I told her.

Beverly started to smile.

"She also is telling me someone just arrived there where she is, something to do with a woman who loves big wigs?"

Beverly started laughing out loud.

"Mrs. Inglebrooks! I used to take care of her! She passed away just a few weeks ago. She would never be seen without this big wig she used to wear."

"Well, your mom wants you to know that Mrs. Inglebrooks says 'Hi' and is thanking you for what you did for her!"

Beverly accepted that and other messages happily, but when her mother started to bring up her passing, Beverly's mood changed.

"Your mom is letting me feel a pain in my chest. Did she pass with a heart attack?"

Beverly started to cry. "Yes."

"But I keep seeing a hospital bed, she didn't pass instantly," I said.

"No, she didn't."

"She's pulling the two of you apart. You were not there when she passed, were you?"

Beverly broke down and started crying.

"My aunt called me and told me my mother had a heart attack. She said she was still alive, but was not going to pull through. I lived 160 miles away from my parents and drove as fast as I could to be with her, but by the time I arrived at the hospital, they told me she had passed," Beverly said through tears. "I never had a chance to say goodbye."

I took a moment to let Beverly's mother respond.

"Well, your mother wants me to ask you a question. You know she's fine, you know she's still very much alive, and you know she is always with you?"

Beverly was nodding her head yes to everything.

"Then why do you feel the need to have said 'goodbye' to her? She says she hasn't gone anywhere, and you know this, she is telling me!"

"I just wanted her to know how much I loved her, and what she meant to me."

"She knows this Beverly, and she loves you so very much. But she wants you to never feel that you needed to say goodbye to her, as she will be a part of you and your families' life . . . always."

I continued, "Your mother is now taking that weight of concern off of your shoulders and is telling you to never feel guilty about it again."

I could see Beverly's shoulders literally lift up as she finally let the weight of this guilt go.

One of the most important messages I would like you to take from this book is to understand that the word "goodbye" need not ever be uttered to someone you know who has passed over. Your loved ones will always participate in all the events that take place in your life.

Be it the happy times or difficult periods that you may go through, those in spirit will always continue to be a part of your life—that you can count on.

17

Living in the past

Memories can be such a wonderful tool to use in our everyday lives. When thinking back on past experiences we've shared with others, we are able to relive those times by flooding our minds with images and emotions we once felt.

But is it possible to abuse memories?

The answer is yes.

I gave a reading to a man named Hank who was very depressed. Hank asked me to connect to his wife Jill, who had passed away a year before. As I stated, not only do I feel the energy of the other side, but of those I'm sitting with as well. I could feel his heavy heart, which actually made a wall of grief that both I and the other side had to break through.

I told Hank to try to relax. We took deep breaths together and I started to feel his wife next to me. Her energy was strong. I could tell she was a loving person, yet had some things on her mind that she was going to get out early in the reading.

"Hank, Jill is telling me you were married for quite a while, fifty-odd years!" I said.

"Yes," Hank replied. "She was my life."

"She is telling me she still is," I said.

"That's hard for me to accept," Hank said.

"Well, she is telling me she wants to prove it. She is saying something about you needing to clean the garage. It's a mess!"

Hank perked up, a bit surprised that he was getting chastised from the other side.

"That is something she would constantly get on me about. I haven't even thought about cleaning it since her passing," Hank said.

"I think you'd better consider it now. She's kind of determined about it!"

Hank replied, "I haven't felt like doing much of anything since she's passed."

"Jill is letting me feel that she is very much concerned about something. Let me see what she is talking about. She is showing me you in bed, and I keep seeing the sun. Do you sleep during the day?" I asked.

"No," Hank said.

"Okay, she keeps showing me this . . . I see the sun, and now I see the moon. I see the sun, and now the moon again, and she shows me you in bed. She says you know what she is talking about."

"Oh, sometimes I don't feel like getting up," Hank said. "What's the point? So I'll stay in bed all day. I just lay there and reminisce about the times we had together."

"Well, she's very concerned about you doing this. What she keeps showing me is her pushing you out of bed. She's not really doing this, but symbolically she is trying to get you up. What this means is, she is saying she wants you to continue living your life."

"That's easier said than done. I can't help the way I feel. I just want her back, and I know she's not coming back. The only things I have left in my life are the memories of her."

I could see Jill shaking her head at this remark. She hugged Hank while doing so.

"Jill is saying this is not true," I replied. "She wants me to tell you she is still with you, and she says you do feel her presence from time to time."

"Sometimes I think I do," Hank said. "But I know that it's just wishful thinking."

Then Jill stopped hugging Hank and, strangely, pulled his right ear as if scolding a child. I paused, and then told Hank of his wife's action.

"Jill wants me to talk to you about that last remark," I said. "She says you better believe she's more than just wishful thinking! She's actually tugging at your ear, like a child."

Hank was very surprised.

"She would do that if she thought I was behaving like a child. I can almost feel her do that at times, but I know it's just my imagination, and that makes me miss her even more."

"Trust your feelings, Hank!" I said. "That's from her, and me. Hank, I can tell you, the love you have for Jill is still shared by you both. It has never stopped. You feel the only way to connect with her, and her love, is through the past. This is just not true. Yes, she did love you in the past, but the fact is, she still loves you . . . now, more than ever. By realizing her love really does continue for you, you will not have to reach into the past to receive it. You have it now, in the present, and always will."

"I have to be honest, Patrick. I really do feel her love coming to me as we're speaking."

"That's because you've opened yourself up to it, and I can tell you, Jill is very happy right now," I said. "And I want you to know, she is looking forward to the new memories she is going to have with you."

"New memories? What does she mean?"

"With Jill continuing to be a part of your life, any experiences you have, good or bad, she, too, will be a part of. By encountering new situations and making new memories for yourself, these will be memories that will be shared by the both of you!"

"I never thought about it like that," Hank said.

I told Hank not to think about the memories of his wife as a missing section of his life, but more of a part that will help him to enjoy his life all the more.

Yes, your loved ones in spirit will continue to be a part of your life, but the important thing is for you to continue living your life. It's wonderful to think back on all the fond memories you have shared with a loved one, as these truly can be gifts. Never use them as a crutch, but as a reason to look toward your future.

Not only do you need to continue to experience all that life has to offer, but your loved ones in spirit want to share them with you as well!

18

Grieving and how it affects your connection

Grieving is a natural state we find ourselves in after the passing of a loved one. To go though this period can be very therapeutic, but why does it seem that some people can go through this process of healing faster than others?

Well, let's break down some of the emotions and stages that one can go through in a grieving state—feelings of confusion, sadness, loss, fear, anger, or guilt.

Before you read on, I want you to reread the emotions above, and associate yourself with any and all that you've had or have been feeling.

Now let me ask you a question. Did you find yourself having the above emotions toward:

- The person who has passed?
- Yourself?
- Or both?

More than likely, your answer is both.

It is not uncommon for people to grieve not only for their loved ones, but also for themselves. This is a natural response. With any passing, there is change and, eventually, acceptance of this change.

- There is change for a spouse if another passes.
- There is change for a child if a parent passes.
- There is change for a parent if a child passes.

I could go on and on, since every individual circumstance is different. Keep in mind, change is not necessarily bad—we make changes in our lives every day, but *we* like to decide any and all change that may occur in our lives—not letting blind faith do it for us. We want to be in control over our own situations.

A loved one's passing forces a change for us, one we usually do not welcome, and with unwanted change comes self-grief.

Believe it or not, most people will go through the process of grieving for a passed loved one in about the same amount of time. Those who take a lot longer continue to grieve, not for the loved one, but for themselves.

❧

Julie and Burt came to see me to connect with their son Danny. Though it had been five years since his passing, it might as well have been yesterday. I could sense the extreme sadness that had become a part of them, and I was anxious to show them their son was still very much alive.

"Danny wants you to know, believe it or not, he still has a beer with his 'old man' while they watch the game together. His words, not mine," I said with a smile.

"Yes, this was something they always did together," said Julie, smiling back.

"Also, he is telling me something about you getting on him about spilling it on your couch. He's laughing about it," I said.

"Any time when there was a good play, Danny would always get excited and jump up, spilling anything he was holding," Burt said.

"Well, he wants you to know that even though you can't see the spills, he's still just as messy as ever!"

"I believe that," Julie said.

"He wants you both to know he is still very much with you and continues his love for you. He is also telling me you have not been noticing any of the signs he is leaving you."

Burt said, "What signs?"

"Let me see what I can get," I said. "He's showing me one thing he does is constantly make your TV turn off. Have you been noticing this?"

"Yes," said Julie. "It's a new television, and I thought I might have to take it back."

"Well you don't have to. He says he'll go a little easier on it from now on. He says you've been asking him for signs, and he is giving them to you. Just keep watching for them, because he is constantly with you."

During this session, Danny came through with other confirmations as well. He had seen what was going on in their lives, and showed how he has been trying to help them.

By the end of the reading, I felt I really had given this couple enough verification to prove that their wonderful son was still very much alive and with them. Usually when someone comes to me for a reading, they would like to have some personal evidence for themselves that their loved ones are in fact still there. I had just given this to them and I hoped that this would help take away some of the grief, but after the reading I could sense continuing sadness with this couple. To me, they felt just as unhappy as they were when they came in. I asked what it was exactly they wanted to hear from their son, and the answer surprised me.

They said they would only be happy again if their son could come home, walk through the door, and be with them physically.

This is an example of how one turns grief inward. These parents had been living in this state for five years, never allowing themselves to heal. Why? They had placed a condition on their healing, one that could never be met. They understood Danny was still with them, and now recognized the different signs he had been giving them, but if they did not get exactly what they wanted, no matter what their son's feelings were, they were going to remain unhappy.

Grief is a heavy emotion, one that brings energy to a very low position. It places a block around a survivor that makes it very hard for loved ones on the other side to penetrate. When people are grieving, they want more than anything to have some type of contact with a loved one who has passed. The problem is, they do not realize what they are doing is the exact opposite of what is needed. For a spirit to be able to communicate with others, those people need to be at a higher level, which can be achieved with happiness or being positive. Once they are capable of dismissing some of the grief they are experiencing, then a stronger connection can be made.

It is certainly natural to be heavy-hearted for ourselves when we are so used to having a physical-to-physical relationship with someone, but once a person passes a new relationship begins—that of being physical-to-spirit.

It is up to you how much you want to develop this relationship!

About eight months later, I received a letter from Julie and Burt. The good news was they had started the healing process, and realized they had been thinking of themselves. They decided to place their focus on knowing their son was still alive and well, and would continue to be with them, in his way—not theirs.

Now you may be asking, *is it okay to not grieve for someone who has passed?*

The answer is yes.

I had a visit from a young lady who had recently lost her grandmother. The feeling I was receiving from her was quite the opposite of that described with the previous couple. She had an incredible lightness and excitement around her that was easy for me to pick up on.

Her grandmother was the first one to come through, and the foremost thing she wanted to talk about was her funeral. This was a little strange to start out with, but of course I went with it. Unlike the solemn feeling that I could receive from a spirit when talking about this subject, her grandmother gave me the feeling of excitement.

"Your grandmother is very thankful for all the love and joy that was given to her at her funeral, she is telling me."

"Really!?" she said.

"Yes, she's letting me feel what she felt, and I have to be honest . . . I am getting a lot of laughing, singing, and clapping."

While stating this, I found myself starting to clap, too. "This was not like an ordinary service, but more like a party," I said.

"Yes!" she replied. "We didn't have a traditional funeral, but more of a celebration and a tribute to her life!"

"Well, it's hard for me to put into words how much this meant and means to her. She wants you to know that she, along with other loved ones on the other side, were dancing and singing right along with everybody!"

"Wonderful! We all felt them around us and knew they were part of this celebration too."

"She's giving me a definite yes!" I said. "Also, did you sing a hymn for her? She is placing a hymnal in your hand and is showing you singing from it, standing by yourself on a platform."

"Yes! It was a hymn she taught me when I was a little girl. I would always sing it to her, so I knew she would enjoy it," she replied.

"She sure did. She loved it!"

As the reading continued, the one continuous message her grandmother gave was how thankful she was that her family knew she was still alive, well, and how they continued to think of her as such.

Again, it is natural to grieve, but the important thing is to get through it. By doing so, you are lifting the heavy blanket of sadness away from you, allowing your loved ones on the other side to connect with you in ways you never thought possible!

Part VI

❧

Your own connection with the other side

Though loved ones on the other side may not be able to come back to you in a physical form, they can and do, however, give evidence of their presence and of their continuous love. The problem is, many people do not recognize the various signs and confirmations their loved ones are leaving.

That is why I would like to help you make a connection yourself with those on the other side.

19

Recognizing their
communications

You may be thinking that if your loved ones have been
connecting with you, you would have noticed.

Want to bet?

Right now, let's try a little experiment. I want you to
close your eyes for about thirty seconds and open them
again. Don't read on—do this now.

Did that feel relaxing? What else did you notice? Probably not very many things, but why?

Because you were not trying to notice anything else.

But what if you did?

Close your eyes again, but this time I want you to notice any and all sounds that you hear, from the loudest to
the softest. Do this now for about a minute.

I would imagine this time you heard much more than
you did the first time you closed your eyes. Why?

Well, think of the environment that is surrounding
you as having different levels—like a jawbreaker has many
layers.

When you were sitting there, obviously the first sounds
you may have noticed would had been the loudest ones,
such as:

- Another person, or other people in your house speaking
- Clocks ticking
- A television or radio playing

But then, once you passed that layer, maybe you heard:

- Your own breathing
- An air conditioner or a fan running
- Sounds from the chair you are sitting in
- Small noises your house may be making

But when you started to listen even more intensely, maybe you heard:

- Birds singing
- Cars passing
- Dogs barking
- Leaves on the tree, rustling in the wind

My point? To show you how much is going on around you that you really never notice—that is, unless you focus on it. Ahhh, there's that word "focus"—and you know what? That really does hold a key to connecting with our loved ones in spirit!

Close your eyes and try the experiment once more. I promise you, each time you do it, you will be more focused, and you will hear more.

The same holds true with noticing the connections of your loved ones in spirit. The more you focus and notice, the more you will have from them!

Now, after reading this chapter many of you will instantly notice what your loved ones have been and are doing for you. For others, it may take more time, as you have to learn how to identify the ways they are connecting with you personally. Don't worry, your loved ones in Heaven are very patient. They will reach out to you lovingly and help you every step of the way.

There are different ways and methods a spirit will connect to you. The following are examples of things you can do, or notice, to recognize the signs of their continuing life.

Dreams

Dreams are one of the easiest ways for a passed loved one to make a connection with you. While awake, your mind is very active, being in a thinking mode. While asleep, this mode or state becomes less dominant, allowing your intuitiveness to take over. In other words, sleeping is another form of meditation. See, and you say you can't meditate!

Being in this state of meditation enables your mind, body, and soul to communicate with spirit beings through your dreams. Understand that not every dream you have of loved ones is actually them connecting and communicating with you, as some dreams can seem odd or nonsensical at times.

When a dream is an actual connection with a loved one, I refer to it as a *visitation*.

A visitation is more powerful and real than a dream. While having a visitation, things will seem normal and tangible in comparison. Your senses are also heightened as if you were actually awake. With a visitation, you tend to remember more of the details, whereas in dreams you can easily forget them. There is also usually some type of message a loved one will convey to you in a visitation.

When I was younger, my dad's mother (whom we call Nanny) once came to me in a visitation to deliver a message to me. In this dream, I was lying in bed and Nanny was walking toward me with an object in her arms. At first, I couldn't make out what it was she was carrying, but I could tell it was something small and furry. As my grandmother continued coming closer to my bed, the object became clearer, Nanny was holding a cat. I couldn't make out any details of the cat because the room was dark. When Nanny finally approached the side of my bed, she bent down and placed the cat on a pillow next to me. As soon as this happened, I woke up, as I literally felt the pressure of the object being placed on the pillow. It was still the middle of the night, and I started pondering what this dream was all about. Finally, I drifted back to sleep.

The next morning this dream was still very fresh in my mind, so I reported to my family what I had experienced the night before. After describing all the details of my dream, at that moment a question was brought up. Where was our cat Ashley?

Ashley was mostly an indoor cat, and none of us had even noticed that she had been missing. We started to look all around the inside of the house for her. Every room was searched, up and down, but Ashley was nowhere to be found. In the search, we did notice a window had been opened and decided she must have gotten out from there. Outside, as we all searched around the house and yard, Kathy heard a slight meow coming from behind a bush below our backyard deck. Going toward the faint cry, Kathy found Ashley lying behind the shrub. We ran over to her and noticed something was wrong. Ashley looked as though she could not focus on anything or anyone, her pupils were enlarged. Ashley, when in a playful mood, likes to climb trees. Although she's pretty good at it, Kathy felt she must have fallen from the tree.

Of course we rushed her straight to the veterinarian. It was exactly what we thought, poor Ashley had fallen and received a concussion. The doctor told us not to worry, she would be as good as new in a couple of days.

So there it was, a dream/visitation from my grandmother letting us know she was not only watching out for us, but for our little Ashley as well.

I have also found that a family member may come through in a visitation to someone who is not even part of the immediate family. Have you ever had this experience yourself? I bet you have. The reason a spirit will convey a message to such a person is that the receiver can sometimes be more objective with the message. This type of connection can give a message more validity, ensuring it is not just a family member's wishful thinking.

With a visitation, don't be surprised to notice a few of the following things:

- Someone who was older when he or she passed looks younger, around the prime of their life.

- Someone who was younger, such as a child, when he or she passed, looks more mature.

- Someone who had a physical deformity is now restored.

- Someone who had passed after a long illness is in perfect health.

- A passed loved one has a certain glow or aura around them.

At first, your loved ones may come to you the way you would have remembered them from this life, but this is for recognition purposes only. As the visitations continue, you will start seeing any changes that have actually occurred to them in spirit, this being their transformation to perfect health and wholeness.

Homework

Keep a pad and pencil or a tape recorder next to your bed. After you awake from having a dream or a visitation, take note of any and all details that you can remember. Don't wait until morning, thinking you'll remember all the details—you probably won't. Do it while it is fresh in your memory. Ask yourself a few of these questions:

- Was there a message in the dream?

- Was the message you received for you or someone else?

- Was anything shown to you symbolically?

- How did your loved one look to you?

If you find that any of the messages you receive may have been for someone else, don't be afraid to pass them along. Though it may not make any sense to you, it may hit home with them! If you are now thinking to yourself, "I can never remember my dreams," don't worry.

If you place yourself in the mindset that this is a type of communication you would like to experience, you will.

Always ask God and your loved ones to help you—they will!

Physical

Love can transcend dimensions, and although we all receive messages from our loved ones on the other side, they can make connections to us in physical ways. Yes, spirits can physically make an object manifest. How? Honestly, I have no idea. But I'm not one to question miracles anyway!

Usually when those on the other side give you signs with inanimate objects, these are going to be with things that had a connection with you, the spirit, or both.

Kathy and I had always enjoyed taking walks around a golf course that is located near our home in Virginia. While on these excursions, we would often come across golf balls lying on the side of the course and would collect them. No, these balls were not in play, nor did we have golfers chasing us! They were just stray balls that some golfers hit out of bounds and left behind. After we collected enough balls to fill our pockets, we would go home and our mom would always try to guess how many we had found that day.

During our mother's illness, we would continue to play this game with her. This made it seem as if she, too, were on the walks with us.

A few months after our mother's passing, Kathy and I were leaving our home in California when we noticed something under our doormat. When Kathy bent down and lifted the mat up to see what it was, to our surprise, we discovered a golf ball. I don't think I have to tell you how amazed by this we were. No one was near our home, nor would even have realized the connection we had with golf balls. We knew instantly where this ball came from—our mom!

We ran back in and called our father in Virginia to let him know of our newly found treasure. To our surprise, he, too, had found a golf ball at his doorstep that very day—three thousand miles away.

There is another way your loved ones will give you physical signs, but you will receive them in a more subtle way. The following is an example.

Carolyn, a good friend of Kathy's and mine, has a sister Catherine who had moved from California to the state of Florida. Catherine was very concerned about this move, since it would put her quite a distance away from her family and friends, whom she loved dearly. Carolyn told her not to worry, that they were only a phone call away, and their father, who had passed, would be with her, as well. One day, while feeling lonely for her loved ones, Catherine noticed a package at her doorstep. This package was delivered to welcome her and her family to their new residence. Besides a few goodies, the package contained information about the local shops, schools, and basic information about her surrounding neighborhood. While Catherine was sorting through all this information, she came across a letter. This was a letter welcoming her, not to her new Florida town, but to Somerville, New Jersey. She thought how odd it was for this letter, which was actually dated many years earlier, to be in her basket. Catherine started contemplating why this letter would be in her basket, when suddenly she made the connection. Her father's hometown was Somerville, New Jersey! With excitement, she got on the phone with her family to tell them the good news. This was just Catherine's father's way of welcoming her to her new home and to let her know that he was there, too!

With a physical sign, don't be surprised to notice a few of the following characteristics:

- It happens when you least expect it.

- Before you noticed it, you were thinking of the spirit a day or two before.

- It happens to more than one person at the same time, but in different places.

- Something previously lost is found.

- Something that meant a lot to the loved one appears out of nowhere.

Homework

The best way for you to make this type of connection is by simply keeping an eye out for the sign. It's important to notice the little things that are going on around you because they may not be as little as you thought.

If you do your part, I can promise you, your signs will be there.

Electricity

Keep in mind, spirits, as energy, are very capable of manipulating things that are electrical. Many times, they will come to you by affecting any and everything that runs on electricity in your home. From making phones and doorbells ring to wreaking havoc with your television sets, spirits will let you know they're around in ways you may not have known. I'm not saying that every time a lightbulb blows out, it's Granddad saying "Hi!" but sometimes, that's exactly what it is.

Though I am fortunate to be able to link with spirits, they will still give me a physical sign when I least expect it.

I was working on the computer one evening, putting the finishing touches on a project that I had been working on, when suddenly I heard a *beep*, and the screen went black! In shock at the now-blank screen in front of me, I looked around and noticed that all of the electricity in the house had gone out! Knowing that I didn't save the last part of my work, I started to fear the worst—everything from that point on was going to be gone! About five seconds later, all the lights came back on, but I was right—part of my project was erased.

As I sat there shaking my head and kicking myself for not saving my project sooner, the spirit of my mother came in. She was smiling and very apologetic about what had just occurred. She indicated to me that Kathy had been very concerned about a problem she had been dealing with and had asked for a sign to let her know that things were going to work out. Hearing this, Mom wanted to just make a light blink that Kathy was sitting by, but she got a little carried away.

I told mom it was certainly okay and thanked her for her message and her love. I asked her jokingly if she could bring back the last part of my project that I hadn't saved.

She said she was in Heaven, not Radio Shack.

I went into the kitchen where Kathy was and told her what had just transpired. Not surprisingly, she, too, had felt Mom's presence and as soon as the lights went on and off, had thanked her for the sign.

I asked Kathy to please make sure not to ask for this type of sign again—while I'm on the computer anyway!

With electricity, don't be surprised to notice a few of the following occurrences:

- The television will go on and off by itself, or frequently change channels without you doing it.

- A spot of color such as purple or green will appear on the TV screen, and may even move around.

- A particular light bulb will constantly burn out, although the socket is fine.

- The phone will ring with no one there.

- The doorbell will ring for no reason.

- Anything electrical will go on, or shut off, without being touched.

Homework

Be specific with your loved ones on the other side. Ask them to give you electrical signs within the next day or two. You may ask them to repeat the same sign, or to give you several different ones.

Again, work with them, and let them know you're watching.

Thoughts

Another way your loved ones will communicate with you is through thought. To put it simply: *every thought you have is not your own.*

Have you ever wondered where that good idea or getting the right answer out of the blue came from? Surprise—it's from your loved ones on the other side! (It's funny though, spirits I have spoken with never seem to claim the bad ideas that we have.)

Telepathically, spirits are able to connect and assist you by giving ideas and answers to some of the questions that you may be pondering. Unfortunately, they are not able to give you all the solutions, because this would take away from certain situations from which you need to learn and spiritually grow. However, they can and will push you in the right direction when able.

I once had a session with a man named Ken, whose wife Lori had passed a couple of years before from cancer. Ken wondered if Lori had seen the newest addition to their family, their ten-month-old granddaughter Carmen. When Ken asked this, Lori started to laugh at him and wanted me to mention "pudding" to him.

A couple of weeks before his reading, Ken was recruited by his son to take care of his wonderful granddaughter. Ken had been pushing for his son and daughter-in-law to enjoy a night out on the town, as it had been a while since they were able to get out of the house. That was one motive Ken had, the other was to have Carmen all to himself.

Ken was keeping a watchful eye on his granddaughter throughout that night, but he kept thinking that he had forgotten to do something. He had followed all the instructions that his son had left, everything from the feeding down to changing the diapers. Not that he needed instructions, mind you, but you know how new parents are. For some reason, Ken kept feeling that something had not been done. As he sat for a moment looking at his "to do" list, a thought came to him—pudding. He didn't know why he kept thinking of it, but the word wouldn't leave his mind. He knew that he had fed some pudding to Carmen earlier, but why was it still on his mind? Trying to figure out what was going on, he went back to check on his grandchild. To his surprise, in the crib was little Carmen, completely covered in chocolate pudding! Ken had left the opened tub of pudding in the crib, and Carmen had gotten hold of it. He couldn't help but burst out laughing! Even though she was a complete mess, Carmen was the cutest thing he had ever seen. He had a feeling that it was his wife Lori who gave him that thought, and he knew she was laughing right along with him! And believe me, she did and was!

With a thought connection, don't be surprised to notice a few of the following:

- Ideas seemingly coming from out of the blue.

- A thought of a loved one in spirit comes to you for no reason.

- If a decision needs to be made, a strong gut instinct or gut feeling takes over.

- You find yourself making a choice that is more like a loved one's than yours, but it works.

Homework

Always ask your loved ones for guidance. If a certain situation comes up where help is needed, use your gut instinct and pay close attention to ideas that seem to just "pop" into your head. More than likely, it'll be the right one—from them!

Ever have days when everything seems to go just right and other days when everything seems to go wrong? It could simply be that on good days you are more receptive to listening to the gut instinct and other days you fight it.

Never doubt that your loved ones on the other side are constantly trying to help you, but you must listen to them as much as possible.

Moving Objects

Spirits have also been known to move around objects that you own from time to time. Not that you will necessarily see items floating around the house, but belongings can have a tendency to become shuffled around. One great example of this is how a spirit will make pictures on the wall crooked. I know, I know, it's an old wives' tale and it may sound corny, but it is a fact. Many times during a reading, a spirit will tell me to acknowledge a picture they may have been playing around with.

I know a woman named Erica who inherited a tea set from her mother. It was an old set, one with a few nicks here and there, and had no real monetary value, but the set was her mother's, and that was what meant the most to Erica.

One day, while Erica was preparing her usual midday tea, she noticed the cup she always used was missing from her set. This was strange, since this was a daily ritual with her, and she knew she had placed the cup back in its spot the day before. Erica looked in all the cabinets, but to no avail. The cup was missing. Yes, there were other cups in the set, but this was the one her mother had always used, making it extra special to her. Erica went ahead and grabbed another cup, thinking she must have just misplaced the other one, and that it would turn up sooner or later.

The next day, Erica, continuing her teatime routine, went to get another cup for her tea and found the missing cup back in its rightful place. At that moment, Erica knew this was a sign from her mother, letting her know she was *still* having tea right along with her!

When a spirit connects with moving objects, don't be surprised to notice a few of the following:

- You lose items that you routinely use, such as car keys, toothbrush, etc.

- Lost items are found.

- Items of a loved one appear out of nowhere.

- Items are rearranged differently.

- Pictures or mirrors are crooked.

Homework

Go around the house and make sure all the pictures, clocks, or whatever you may have hanging on your walls are completely straight. Now, ask for your loved ones on the other side to move something on your wall in the next day or two. I'll bet during that time period you will be surprised at what you find. The more you notice, the more you will have these types of signs. Some of you may be thinking that this seems silly. Don't our loved ones on the other side have more important things to do than move a picture or jiggle keys?

Keep in mind that these are all connections, no matter how small they may seem, and any communication with our loved ones is important to you as well as to them!

Feeling

Another powerful connection, one that a lot of people tend to brush off, is actually *feeling* your loved ones with you.

Have you ever had the sensation of a passed loved one being in the same room with you and just brushed it off as imagination or wishful thinking? Well stop doing that! It's not your imagination, nor is it wishful thinking.

It is you, actually sensing your loved one's presence!

My sister Kathy has always had a talent for baking. Even when she was little, she would always help our mother in the kitchen. Kathy has also always felt the spirit of our grandmother Mary around when she was cooking, yet never told anyone this. Anytime she would get stuck on remembering a recipe, she would always ask Mary for help. One day I was hanging around the kitchen while Kathy was making us some goodies. While I was watching her do her thing, and, of course, staying out of her way, I noticed an image following Kathy around the kitchen and found out it was Mary. Without telling Kathy who I was noticing, I asked her if she felt anyone around her. She replied that she had been thinking about our grandmother Mary and feeling her presence around her all day in the kitchen. Kathy had been making an old family recipe for a bread-crumb nut cake and couldn't remember one ingredient. To herself, she asked Mary what it was, and the ingredient popped into Kathy's head. She knew it was Mary who gave her the answer, and I confirmed it was!

I can guarantee there has been a time when you were alone in a room, but suddenly felt someone come in. Turning around to see if you were right, you found you were. It wasn't the fact you saw them, nor even heard them come in. It was that you felt their entrance, you connected with their energy, and by doing this, you probably didn't even give it a second thought. If you're a parent, there may have been many times you felt your child, when he or she was sneaking up behind you. Also, if you have more than one child, I would venture to say you could tell which one it was without even seeing them. How? By connecting with their energies, their souls.

So, by understanding that you have been and are able to connect with living people's energy/souls, it's really not so hard to believe you can also connect with spirits!

Trust your feelings.

When you connect with a loved one in spirit by feeling, don't be surprised to notice a few of the following:

- The feeling of someone watching you.
- The feeling of someone standing right beside you.
- The calming feeling of safety and well-being from a spirit.
- A pressure or slight ringing in your ear from the presence of their energy.
- The hair on the back of your neck standing up as their energy comes in the room.

Homework

With this connection, some of you will be more sensitive than others. The more sensitive ones will be able to recognize immediately the energy of a spirit and who it is. Others may feel a spirit presence, but not know for sure who it is. In this case, set up some guidelines for your loved ones. An example of this would be to tell a spouse who is on the other side to connect with you on your left side, maybe allowing you to feel their energy around your arm or shoulder. Tell a grandparent who wants to make a connection to come on your right side and send energy or pressure to your hand. It's up to you how you want them to connect to you. Feel free to give those on the other side instructions on how they can help you to identify them. They will happily comply. They know this is a new experience for you and want to help alleviate any confusion, because they want you to recognize who is who when they come for a visit. Don't be afraid to set up familiar guidelines for them.

Again, the more you know who is connecting to you, the happier they, too, will become!

Psychometry

Along the same lines as feeling, another way of connecting with a loved one's energy is through psychometry. I would bet that many of you have held an object that belonged to a passed loved one and had not only thoughts of that person come to you, but feelings as well.

This is due in part to the fact that the person's energy is still with that object. Because our body is a shell for our soul, and our soul is energy, we may have a tendency to leave parts of it behind. It's sort of like an energy fingerprint. Sounds crazy? Before you answer, let me ask you a few questions.

- Have you ever been antique hunting for a certain piece of furniture, and when you finally thought you'd found the perfect piece, it just didn't feel right?

- The same example can be used with a piece of jewelry, or even old clothes. You held these items in your hand, and for some reason, you decided against them.

Or the opposite:

• You fall in love or you are comforted when coming across any of the above objects, not that they are your style, but they just feel right.

If you said yes to any of the questions above, guess why? Because you are sensitive to energy, you just may never have realized it. Here's another example of Kathy connecting with energy.

One time we, along with a couple of friends, went on a tour of the *Queen Mary*. This marvel of a ship is dry-docked in Long Beach, California, and we thought it would be fun to go aboard. Kathy and I had been before, but wanted to enjoy it with our friends. It was a beautiful Sunday morning when we arrived, and the ship (and it is called a ship, not a boat as director of the movie *Titanic*, James Cameron, once corrected me—but that's another story) is docked just off the Pacific Ocean. When you board the *Queen Mary*, the first thing you admire is her size. It's overwhelming! You can't help but think back on how this huge vessel would carry the world's most renowned passengers while sailing back and forth from Europe to America. This ship is full of history and stories all its own.

As we went aboard and walked on the main deck, Kathy started to experience a strange sensation. We had been on ships before, including this one, but for some odd reason, Kathy felt as if the boat was sinking. We all knew this could not be, since it has been docked for some time, and it wasn't going anywhere. While we walked around the main deck, this feeling seemed to come over Kathy in only one area of the floor. She actually had to hold on to a railing at one point, stating that she felt as if she were falling to the bottom of the ocean. When we walked away from this area, the sinking sensation would leave her. After making sure Kathy was fine and could continue, we went ahead with our friends on the tour.

As we descended to the deck right below the one we were on, to our surprise, there was a special exhibit. There, actual relics were exhibited that had been salvaged from the *Titanic*.

Kathy had experienced the sinking feeling on the deck right above the *exact spot* where these relics were being displayed.

With psychometry in mind, think about an object and consider the following questions:

- What emotions do you receive from holding this object? Good? Bad? Happy? Sad?

- Do you see any colors in your mind?

- Do you receive any images when holding the object?

- Is there love attached to the item?

- Was the owner of the item young or old?

- Is the item connecting to a certain holiday or event that may have been important to the owner?

Homework

Have a friend or a relative give you a piece of jewelry from a passed loved one. Once you have it in your hands, take note of what you receive. Take your time and feel the object. Record what your first impressions are. Don't second-guess yourself or try to talk yourself out of the information that is coming into your mind. Test yourself, you may be more sensitive than you realize.

Seeing

Besides visitations, is it really possible to see a loved one who has passed over to the other side?

You bet it is!

But you have to be open to what *seeing* loved ones in spirit is really like. If you have certain expectations, and want them to come to you in your own way, you will more than likely be disappointed. Your loved ones do come to you, but you have to be open to seeing them *their* way.

To see a spirit, your mind has to be in a relaxed state. This could happen before you drift off and fall asleep, or as you awake in the morning. Your brain is not in that *thinking* mode, but more in an *intuitive* state. When one sees a spirit, it usually happens in a split second, and you may toss it off as imagination. Sitting in your favorite place watching TV or reading, you may have noticed someone or something out of the corner of your eye. This may appear as a dark or light shadow, or a movement of some sort. When you turn to see who or what it is, it disappears.

While watching television or reading, your mind is in a meditative state, which allows your intuitiveness to open up. By seeing this image, and turning toward it, trying to view it with your physical eyes, you automatically turn off that intuition. Then what happens? The image disappears. But don't think that the image/spirit really goes anywhere, it doesn't. It's just that you are no longer seeing it. More than likely, it is a passed loved one who is visiting and watching your soaps with you!

I met with a woman named Dorothy who had lost her pet dog Sammy. Every night, when Dorothy and her husband Greg would settle in for the evening, Sammy would follow right along, lying in between their chairs.

Eventually, due to old age, Sammy passed away. Again, any pet owner knows the grief that can come from a pet's passing.

As time went on, Dorothy was able to let go of some of her grief by thinking about all the good times that she had with Sammy, not realizing that the good times were in fact going to continue.

After awhile, Dorothy started to notice something strange. Out of the corner of her eye, she would keep seeing movement, just as she had as if Sammy were there. But when she looked down to see exactly what it was, nothing was there. Dorothy, of course, passed this vision off as her imagination.

One evening, Greg mentioned to Dorothy that he thought he needed to have his eyes checked out. When Dorothy asked what type of eye trouble he was having, Greg replied that for some reason, he kept seeing a moving shadow around her chair. Hearing this, Dorothy excitedly told him that she, too, had been seeing the same visions! Because both of them had seen this image, they knew exactly what, or who, it was—Sammy, still running around the house! All of this was later confirmed in a reading that I had with the couple.

When seeing a spirit, don't be surprised to notice a few of the following sights:

- You notice a shadow out of the corner of your eye, only to have it disappear when you turn to look at it.

- A light streak brushes by you quickly.

- A mist appears and then goes away instantly.

- Seeing flashing lights or dots in the dark.

Homework

Next time you see an image out of the corner of your eye, without turning, ask yourself the following: who do you feel it is? What feelings are connected with this sighting? Do you smell any type of scent as well? Does anything you receive relate to a loved one who has passed? This one takes practice, but as I've mentioned before, the more you do this, the better you will become at it.

Smelling

If a certain scent or fragrance was associated with a loved one before they passed to the other side, he or she will certainly help make their presence known to you by using it.

Spirits have the ability to produce scents such as perfume, cologne, tobacco, or flowers in order for you to know that they are still around. Some of you are nodding your heads yes right now as you read because you can relate to this.

Spirits at times will try to make you use any and all of your senses to recognize them, including smell.

Working in a pizza business for forty years, Al used to come home from the shop smelling like dough every day. This was something his wife Gina had grown accustomed to. She fell in love with this pizza boy, thirty-eight years ago, and had come to love everything about him, including the smell of freshly baked pizzas.

After his passing, it was difficult for Gina to get rid of all of Al's material things, such as his shirts, shoes, and other clothing items. She would often go into the closet and wrap herself in these items as a reminder of him. Gina felt a connection by doing so. After her father's passing, Gina's daughter insisted that Gina move from the city to live with her and her husband in Connecticut, which Gina did. It was hard to leave her life and start a new one, but she felt it was the right thing to do.

Every night, Gina would pray to Al to watch over her and their family. Her prayers were answered. One night, after taking Gina out to dinner and a movie, the family came home and called it a night. Gina went to her room and turned in. That night she was awakened with the familiar fragrance of pizza. She thought maybe her daughter was cooking late for her husband, but to her surprise, no one was even up. She knew she wasn't mistaken about this pungent smell—it was a smell she had known for many years.

Gina's daughter saw a light coming from the other room and got out of bed thinking something was wrong. When she approached her mother, she, too, could smell the scent of a pizza—not just any pizza, but the ones Al use to make!

They hugged each other in joy, knowing that Al was still around them, making pizza. He had confirmed with Gina that no matter where she lived, he would always be with her.

With a scent connection, don't be surprised to notice a few of the following:

- Floral scents coming from nowhere.
- Smelling food that you associate with a loved one in spirit.
- Smelling any scent that instantly connects you to a loved one in spirit.
- Having a problem and the scent of a passed loved one actually helping you calm down.

Homework

Ask loved ones to help you to connect with them through scent. If you know of a scent you would instantly recognize as coming from them, ask them for it. If they were not associated with a particular aroma, request they produce a floral smell for you. Keep in mind, the scent may just last a second, a minute, or possibly longer, but always enjoy it!

It's a gift of communication, and the more you recognize it, the more it will happen.

Photographs

Spirits appearing in photographs are providing a remarkable, yet often unnoticed, way of making contact with you. When we are in the picture-taking mood, it's usually during family gatherings such as holidays, birthdays, and anniversaries—anything and everything we celebrate. During these times, people have a tendency to feel their loved ones in spirit joining in the celebration. Not only are they joining in, but many of them will step right into the pictures that are being snapped!

A woman named Helen came to see me one day for a reading. Her husband Peter had come through and told her that he had attended the birthday party that was just thrown for her. She told me that she had felt his presence and was happy to hear this confirmation. Peter also wanted her to know he was in the picture with her. At this point, Helen was confused. She agreed that pictures had been taken, but she didn't notice anything unusual. Peter told her to just take another look at the photos of the party.

A few weeks later I received a letter in the mail from Helen. She was extremely excited because she had spotted the picture to which Peter was referring. Helen included a copy of the picture, and said her husband's image could clearly be seen. As I looked at the picture, I certainly saw Helen sitting by a window, but I couldn't see any sign of Peter. I knew spirits can be seen in pictures in many way, varying from an energy bubble appearing on the photograph to energy smears that will make part of the picture look blurry. In this photo, I couldn't make out Peter to save my life, but if Helen saw her dear husband in it, that's all that mattered. About six months later, Kathy and I were lecturing in Los Angeles. After we finished, and while we were meeting those in attendance, a woman came up and identified herself as Helen, the one who had sent the photo to me. I was happy to see her, and remembered her face from the photo she had sent. She asked me if I had noticed her husband in the picture. I had to be honest with her, and said that I looked and looked at the photo, but couldn't make out what she saw. With that, Helen pulled out the photo and gave it to me to look at again, but this time told me to turn the picture sideways.

There it was, right in front of me, camouflaged in the blinds she was sitting in front of, the faint face of a man. The image in the photograph was not solid by any means, but more of a mass of light and shadows that did form a face.

I said laughingly, "Why didn't you tell me to turn it sideways?"

Helen, laughing also, took out another picture of her husband, this one taken while he was alive so that I could compare the image to the real person. I can honestly say that Peter was not camera shy—here or there.

Spirits in photographs can come across in numerous ways. They can be seen in the form of light energy circles or bubbles that seem to float around. They can also appear as a light smear that you may have assumed was under- or over-development with a particular picture. Or an image of a spirit can be even more detailed, with physical attributes actually visible.

With a photo of a spirit, don't be surprised if you notice a few of the following:

- A bright dot or dots appearing in a photo.

- A light smudge or smear that seems to be floating in a picture.

- Any shadows that look out of place.

- Actual translucent images of a passed loved one, in whole or in part.

- Any sort of glow that may be around or beside an individual.

Homework

Take out all of your photo albums and other pictures. This can be done when you are alone, but it can be a lot of fun having friends and loved ones join in! Taking your time, examine all the pictures with a fine-tooth comb. See if you can notice any type of unusual images you may not have observed before. Look for lights, shadows, smears, dots, even figures.

You may be surprised at what you'll find.

Animals

Animals are another wonderful and noticeable way our loved ones in spirit connect with us. Since animals are very sensitive, they are able to not only see and hear spirits, but also take instructions from spirits as well.

Take Marty, for instance—a man who is what you would call an all-out bird lover. Marty's parents never could understand how, as a child, he could have such a knack of finding birds that were somehow hurt or wounded and bringing them home. He felt it was his duty to look after them and nurse them back to health. When Marty would walk through his front door, cupping his hands, his parents knew the "doctor was in."

As an adult, Marty's love for birds didn't end. Though he didn't go scouting around for hurt ones any longer, he did own a few that he loved dearly. One was a parrot named Jimmy. Marty had named it after his father because it reminded him of his dad. He also knew naming a bird after his father would bait his dad every time they would come over.

But that's okay; Jim would get his son back. Every time they came over, Jim would go to the bird and try to teach him a common curse word. The family really didn't know what was funnier, the bird trying to mimic what Jim was saying, or just watching Jim saying the "s" word over and over to a bird.

Jim finally succeeded, and anytime he came over, he would have the best time making the bird say that word. The funny thing was, Jim was the only one who could make the bird say it. No matter how much others tried, the bird would respond only to Jim.

Marty's father passed away from a heart attack some years later. After the funeral, Marty had a gathering at his home because he did not want his mother to have to deal with and worry about everything. While the family assembled, reminiscing and telling stories about Jim, at that very moment Jimmy the bird started yelling his special word, out loud, over and over again. Every one looked up with amazement and surprise. There was no one near the bird, and in fact, the cage was covered up so as not to disturb him.

They knew at that moment it was Jim playing around as he always had, letting the family know that he was just fine, and still teasing the bird!

Always notice how your pets act around you. I have been told by many spirits how they will make their dogs bark or how their cats will watch them walking around. Also, it may not just be a family pet they will affect. They will make a certain bird come to you—insect, squirrel rabbits—anything that may have a meaning for you.

With animals, don't be surprised to notice a few of the following:

- A pet looking as if they are watching something or someone who's not there.

- A dog barking at nothing, a cat meowing at nothing, or any other animal making an unprovoked noise.

- A pet hanging around a loved one's favorite place, chair, room, etc.

- A pet staring for a while at a picture or spot on a wall for no reason.

- Any animal that seems to come out of nowhere, catching your eye.

Homework

If you have pets, pay attention and observe when they start acting in a strange or an unusual manner. Notice if this happens during the same time of day, or in a certain place in a room, or outside. Also, if you don't have a pet, notice other animals that seem to come your way for no reason at all.

Animals are very sensitive and usually don't mind helping with a connection between you and your loved one!

Creativity

Anything that is done creatively, be it writing, music, drawing, cooking, planting, etc., can also include connecting with loved ones in spirit.

When someone is in the creative mode, this is yet another way of meditating. I bet those of you who are creative find that you tune out the rest of the world while doing something creative. Being in this state is an excellent time for connecting to the other side.

Landscape painting was Sandra's way of relaxing. After a hard and hectic week, she would look forward to the time where she was able to be by herself and work out her stresses by painting a beautiful landscape. Sandra always thought it amazing how fast time passed by as she made a blank canvas come alive with the colors and shapes of her surroundings.

One gloomy, rainy day, Sandra was unable to go out and paint due to the inclement weather, so she decided to just make up a scene in her mind. She sat there wondering if it should be a landscape or an ocean beach scene, when suddenly she felt the urge to paint a farm. She had never painted a farm before, so she thought why not?

Brush stroke after brush stroke, the image of the farm she had in her mind became a reality on canvas. It consisted of a barn, of course, some livestock, and what she thought was kind of unusual, a farmhouse that had two front entrances.

Nearing the end of her painting, Sandra's doorbell rang. Answering it, she found her mother had come over for a visit. Her mother was a big supporter of Sandra's art and, noticing she had been painting, asked to see her newest work. Sandra took her mother to the easel and was surprised at her mother's expression. Sandra asked if she didn't like the painting. Her mother looked at Sandra with astonishment and asked her why she had painted *this house*. Sandra replied she really didn't know, it was just a picture she had in her mind. Sandra's mother explained with excitement that the farmhouse she had painted was where she lived as a little girl. It didn't exist any longer, and she knew Sandra couldn't have known what it looked like since there were no pictures of it, until now.

When being creative, don't be surprised if you notice a few of the following circumstances:

- The feeling of someone beside you.
- Ideas, when needed, seem to come from nowhere.
- You have several different styles of creativity in your work.
- You look at the finished work and know that others helped you because you couldn't possibly have done this work by yourself.

Homework

This is a connection that will come when you are in the creative mode. When in this state, try not to concentrate too hard, but allow your loved ones in spirit to give you ideas or direction on where your project should go.

Make sure those who are helping you are creative themselves, as you never know what you might end up with!

Music

Music is an excellent way for a loved one in spirit to connect with you, and there are several ways this can happen. One common way is when you find yourself humming a song to yourself, for no reason, but when you catch yourself doing so, you know it was a song that meant something to your loved one, or possibly to both of you. Certainly there would be no reason for you to be humming it, but you were. Why?

Just as with hearing thoughts and words from a loved one in spirit, they can also give you thoughts of music.

Another way a spirit will utilize music is by actually arranging for you to hear a song that means something to you. This would be either through the radio, television, or anything else that is actually audible. Now you may be asking, how could this be? Well, it really isn't that hard to accept. Many times you may be riding in your car and all of a sudden you feel the need to turn on the radio and a song happens to be playing that reminds you of someone. Did the DJ know you would be listening at that time and decide to play it for you? No, but your loved one did! Because those in spirit would know when a particular song might be played, they could also inspire you with the thought of turning on the radio just in time to hear it. Hearing this song will make a connection between the two of you.

I once met a man named Olen. Olen's wife, Patricia, had passed from surgical complications and he wanted to know if she was all right. Patricia did connect with me and assured him she was. In fact, she was in perfect health. Patricia gave Olen confirmations about things she had been seeing and doing with him since her passing. During his reading, I asked Olen if he had noticed the sign of music she had left him. He thought for a moment and said nothing rang a bell. Patricia told me to tell him that she was the one who told him to get some gas.

I had no idea what that meant, or how it was connected with music, when all of a sudden Olen got a big smile on his face. On the way over to his session, being somewhat early, Olen decided he had time to get some gas. When he was standing at the pump, he heard the song "Don't Worry, Be Happy." He hated that song, but hearing it reminded him of Patricia and the way she used to always tease him with it.

She still is.

With a music connection, don't be surprised to notice a few of the following:

- You turn on the radio and a special song will be playing.
- For no reason, a song will be in your head, and it brings back memories of a loved one.
- Someone with you starts to hum or sing a tune that connects and says it just popped into his or her head.

Homework

When driving in your car, and before you turn on your radio, ask a loved one in spirit what song will be playing or will be coming on while you are listening. Don't tell him or her what you want played, let them tell you what it will be, and listen to the first answer that comes to you!

The more you do this, the more you can connect with a loved one in spirit with music!

Nature

Just as spirits can connect with our human energies, they can connect with nature. It's a known fact that all living things on the Earth have a life force around them. From a blade of grass to the tallest tree, everything has energy and, in some ways, a soul.

After the passing of her mother, Elizabeth had the task of putting her mother's affairs in order. Jane's passing was not a shock by any means, as she had had cancer for some time, and Elizabeth felt it was a blessing her mother was now with her father.

While going through and deciding what to do with what, Elizabeth noticed a small ivy plant she had given her mother before she went into the hospital. It had died from a lack of watering. Not thinking anything of it, Elizabeth just set it to the side and continued packing her mother's belongings.

About another week went by, and Elizabeth had just about cleared out everything in her mother's house. While going through room by room, making sure everything was empty, Elizabeth was shocked. Behind a door where she had left her mother's dead plant, there it stood completely alive, flourishing as if it had been watered the whole time.

Elizabeth's mother still had a green thumb—even in Heaven.

With nature, don't be surprised to notice a few of the following:

- Rapid growth of a flower or plant.
- Cut flowers staying fresh longer than usual.
- Something having a stronger scent than usual.

Homework

Ask loved ones in spirit to give you an exact nature sign. If there is a favorite plant, flower, tree, or shrub, ask them to give you a sign with it. The key is to notice anything unusual or out of the ordinary.

Sounds

Things that go bump in the night—sounds frightening, doesn't it? It can be if you don't know what or where those sounds might be coming from. Once you do understand how your loved ones in spirit use sound, those sounds can be comforting!

Sometimes it is much easier for a spirit to make a sound with something instead of other types of connections. These sounds do not actually come from spirits, but will be produced by them with something in or around your home.

I had a reading where I connected with a man named Mark. Mark's brother James was sitting in front of me as I was giving him confirmations from Mark. James understood everything that was coming through and was excited about all the things Mark was telling him. During the reading, James asked why he hadn't had his own connections with Mark. I sat there and waited for Mark to respond. Mark told me to tell James he had been connecting with him, but James didn't realize it. James asked how Mark was doing this. Mark started laughing and answered, "Who in the hell else would be walking up and down your stairs in the middle of the night?" James got a happy but shocked look on his face. He had been hearing the creaking of his steps, but just took it as the house settling. Mark told James that wasn't the case anyway and to continue to listen for him because, frankly, he liked doing it!

Typical sounds to listen for would be:

- Wooden floors creaking.
- The sound of doors and windows shutting.
- Thumping sounds on walls, ceilings, and floors.
- Footsteps when no one else is walking.

Homework

Notice and keep track of any sounds or noises you start to hear in or around your home. See if these sounds will repeat themselves and how often. Also keep track to see if these sounds come when you are thinking about a loved one in spirit.

Though you may not hear "Boo" from them, you will hear something, I assure you!

Taste

Take a moment to think about your favorite meal. Whatever it is, close your eyes and imagine it right in front of you. While imagining it, you can almost taste it, right? But the food isn't really in front of you, so how can you almost taste it? It's because your taste buds are one of your senses, and taste is another sense a spirit can connect with.

Kel was not in any way, shape, or form an expert chef, but he did like to play around in the kitchen from time to time. While reminiscing with his father one day, a dish his mother used to make came up in the conversation, one he had long forgotten about.

There was no real name for this recipe, they just called it "Bologna Surprise." His father said that as a child Kel used to beg his mother to cook it for him all the time. Though Kel had totally forgotten about Bologna Surprise, he decided to try to duplicate it for old times' sake. Going into the kitchen, he placed some bologna in the pan, added cheese, put some ketchup on it, along with a dash of this and a dash of that. And there it was, Bologna Surprise, just like he remembered it, or so he thought. When Kel sat down to eat it though, something was wrong—it was not at all as he remembered it. It looked the same, but it sure didn't taste anything like Kel remembered it tasting.

The next morning, while Kel was waking up, he noticed a strange taste in his mouth. He wasn't sure what it was, but it really tasted like garlic. But that couldn't be, as Kel had brushed his teeth the previous evening, and besides, he didn't even eat anything with garlic in it the day before. But Kel knew the taste of garlic, he loved it. So not thinking anything of it, he went on and started his day. While passing through the kitchen, it hit him like a ton of bricks. Garlic! This was what was missing from his Bologna Surprise! He had forgotten that his mother would always put garlic in it, because he couldn't get enough of it!

Kel may have forgotten the recipe, but his mother hadn't, and what better way of reminding someone about garlic than through their taste buds!

With taste, don't be surprised to notice a few of the following:

- A flavor in your mouth for no reason.

- If you are shopping in a grocery store, you taste the flavor of something you need to purchase.

- You don't have an appetite, then all of a sudden you have a craving or taste for something.

Homework
This is one that you will just have to notice when it happens. If, for no apparent reason, you start to notice a flavor or taste that reminds you

of a food or a meal that you connect with someone, it is that person who is actually connecting with you!

With this type of connection, just hope your loved ones in spirit are good cooks!

Voice

Can spirits really vocally speak with you? Yes. Again, this is a connection that many people will attribute to their imaginations. This type of connection is similar to having one with thoughts, but instead, you actually hear their voices, rather than hearing your own. When spirits communicate in this fashion, they are using your inner ear, the one you use when you're talking with yourself. You can sit there and have a whole conversation with yourself and not think twice about it, but if you start hearing a loved one's voice inside your head, you may feel it is just wishful thinking. If most people would just listen to what that loved one had to say, they would find out it is not.

Donald was driving home one evening after a hard day at work, and, as always, wasn't in any rush to get home. Since the passing of his wife Georgia a year earlier, he would usually take the long way home and reminisce at certain spots he and his wife frequently visited. While driving by these places, Donald would often feel Georgia's spirit with him, as if she were still sitting right beside him in the car.

This particular evening, Donald had an urge to stop and take a break at one of the locations. While sitting there, like always, he would start thinking of past conversations that he and his wife had shared. But something unusual started to happen, Donald started to hear a conversation, but one that seemed to be taking place now, as if Georgia were actually speaking to him. He was hearing her tell him not to ignore the pain he had been feeling in his arm that day and to go to the hospital right now. Donald wasn't sure why he would be remembering this conversation, since it was one that had never taken place. The fact was, a pain he had been feeling that day had annoyed him. The tone he was hearing in Georgia's voice was one of determination.

Donald would hear this tone only when Georgia was being firm about something. He felt he should listen to this message and see if there was anything to this pressure he was feeling in his arm. He made the right decision. Several arteries of his heart were blocked—he needed to have them cleared that very moment. With the proper care, Donald overcame his heart ailment. He also knew it was his wife who made him go to the hospital, that she was still looking out for him.

With a hearing connection, don't be surprised to notice a few of the following:

- Are you hearing something about yourself?

- Are you hearing information about someone else?

- Were you even thinking about this person when you heard their voice?

- The voice is audibly different from your own.

Homework
When you feel you may be hearing your loved ones, never push it away as your imagination. You may hear sporadic words or even sentences, but pay attention to everything.

By understanding how your loved ones in spirit have been connecting with you, you will notice a great deal more from them. If any of these connections make you uncomfortable, simply tell your loved ones not to do them. It is always your choice.

By recognizing any or all of these connections, you will be able to continue your relationship with your loved ones who are on the other side.

20

Meditation

In the past, meditation has been perceived as being done by someone who is sort of "way out there" or "earthy." That is not the case at all! Everyone and anyone can and does meditate, no matter what walk of life they're in or what kind of time they may have on their hands.

Did you know that you meditate at times without even realizing it?

I remember, as a child, I would lie in my backyard for hours at a time and watch the clouds pass by. While lying there, I loved to figure out what image a cloud was making before it changed its shape into something else.

At the time, I was actually meditating, though I didn't know it.

Some activities that you're doing every day that involve meditating, and that you may not be aware of could be:

- Driving a car.
- Listening to music.
- Watching nature.
- Reading.
- Taking a relaxing bath.

- Painting.
- Writing.
- Exercising.

The list could go on and on, and you may be asking yourself, "How can I be meditating while doing some of these things?" Easy. While your mind is concentrating on various activities, your subconscience is allowed to come through.

If you enter into meditation with a completely open mind, it could be one of the greatest gifts you could give to yourself. Meditating allows you to let go of all the stress and anguish of everyday living while energizing your mind and body.

It can also help with the connection to your own loved ones on the other side.

I know, you're going to tell me you've tried to meditate, but you just cannot stop thoughts from coming in while you're relaxing. That's okay, it happens to everyone. You'll get past this. The key to remember is: the more you practice meditating, the better you will become, and the better you become, the more benefits you'll receive from it.

In the following chapters, I am going to describe a couple of mediations you might like to try. Though they are used for different purposes, both work with the energies that surround your body. I can promise you this: once you learn how to work with these energies, you will be amazed at the results you will receive!

Here are some rules of thumb before you begin:

1. You may meditate as often as you like, but more does not necessarily mean better. It's quality, not quantity that counts.

2. Try to find a quiet time to do your meditation. Having the kids run around the house, or the dog scratching to get out is definitely a no-no. Just make sure that when you start, you will not be interrupted.

3. Take the phone off the hook!

4. Find a nice comfortable place to do your meditation. If you have a favorite chair, great. Don't feel you have to sit on the floor—that is, unless you want to.

5. Wear something comfortable. While meditating, you never want your mind to be distracted by clothes that feel awkward or binding.

6. When you begin, make sure your back is straight, your feet are flat against the floor, and your hands are on your lap. A lot of people like to have their palms facing up, but do whatever feels comfortable. If this means sitting on the floor with your legs crossed—go for it.

Breathing is very important while meditating. I know you can breathe because you are breathing as you read this. Breath will cleanse and energize the body. It sustains life and purifies by getting all the toxins out as well.

Here is a disciplined way you can breathe while bringing yourself into a meditative state.

1. Close your eyes and begin by inhaling deeply through your nose for the count of four.

2. Once there, hold the breath for the same count of four.

3. Once done, exhale through your mouth for the count of six. (Make sure when you exhale that you push as much of the air out of your lungs as possible.)

4. Repeat each of the above steps six to eight times.

5. Make sure you do not do your controlled breathing too quickly. Take your time! If you tend to feel a little dizzy, just stop at that point.

21

Magnet meditation

Have you ever felt when you left someone that he or she was still with you?

That is because they are!

As we are all Spirit first, we have a tendency to pick up and take with us other people's energies. Not that you can see this, but you certainly can feel it. Of course, some of you do this more than others, depending on how sensitive you are. This first meditation is one I call the "Magnet Meditation." It is designed to do two things:

1. Lift off any energy that does not belong to you.

2. Retrieve and restore all energies that belong to you.

I would suggest that you read over all the following steps first to become familiar with what to do.

Step 1:
Do all that is written after step one!

Step 2:
Place feet flatly on the floor, hands resting on your thighs, and close your eyes. (Of course, open and close them after reading each step.)

Step 3:

While doing the breathing exercise in chapter 20, I want you to imagine a bright white light just above your head. As you are breathing in, picture and feel this light surrounding you and entering you through the crown of your head. With each breath, you can actually feel your energy increasing. Your body starts to energize as it begins to fill and is surrounded with positive energy and love. Now, take a few moments to just feel and enjoy these changes that are happening to you.

Step 4:

While surrounded by this wonderful white light, picture a giant magnet over your head.

Step 5:

As soon as you feel the magnet is in place, concentrate on how it starts to pull away all the energies that are not yours. Think about the people that you recently have come into contact with, and have the magnet remove all of their energy from you, sending it back to them with love. (You're probably feeling tingly all over by now as you actually feel this energy being lifted from your body.) Sense all the stressful energy being pulled from around your feet, legs, arms, back, shoulders—your entire body.

Do this for about two minutes. Let the magnet do the work.

Step 6:

Once done, have the magnet disappear. Then picture a warm, golden light coming from above, and have it penetrate the top of your head. As it does this, you start to feel it travel down from your head to your chest area. Then it cascades down through your arms and stomach. The light then flows down your thighs and legs and enters your feet. It tingles and feels light. You feel renewed. This is your energy coming back to you, coming from where you might have left it. Whether it was the places you went to or the people you may have come in contact with, have all of this wonderful energy become a part of you. The light then starts to travel back up the body. As it reaches the top of your head again, picture the golden light overflowing and cascading down and around the outside of your entire body. You feel very energized as this is taking place, but most of all you feel complete again, refreshed.

Do this step for about two or three minutes. Once completed, see how different you feel. More than likely, you will feel lighter and I will bet you have a smile on your face! Good job!

I would suggest doing this meditation after a stressful day or coming in contact with someone who gave you tension for whatever reason.

I promise, the more you do this, the more you will receive the benefits from it.

22

The garden meditation

The next meditation is a guided meditation designed to help you in opening your chakras and to connect with Spirit. You may be asking: what in the world are chakras? Chakras are energy points that run from the base of your spine to the top of your head. Opening these points will allow you to be more intuitive with yourself and with those on the other side.

A good idea would be to read the meditation below out loud while recording yourself. I would also suggest playing some soft music in the background to help set the mood. After you record yourself, you will be able to use this meditation over and over again to open yourself up and connect with your loved ones in spirit who are around you.

Now let's begin this beautiful meditative journey.

Picture yourself walking in a lush and fragrant garden, one that is very peaceful and calm. The wind is warm and gentle as it brushes against you, and you hear the birds singing in the trees surrounding you. Looking around

and seeing how beautiful everything is, you notice a pathway just ahead of you. As you start down this path, you come across a lovely rosebush. The sweet smell of all the blossoms fills the air, and you pull one of the buds toward you. You notice that the bud is just beginning to open, and you see that it is the deepest red you've ever seen, as if all the rubies in the world have been taken and condensed into this one rose. As you breathe in the perfume from this rose, the color, so illuminating, beams around your entire body.

Putting the rose down, you turn and notice a table with crystal dishes on it. As you walk over and approach it, a sparkling bowl filled with big, bright, juicy oranges catches your eye. As your hand reaches down and picks up an orange, you notice that it has the color of the sun—bright and glowing. When you start to stare at its vibrant color, you actually feel its glow wrapping around you like a warm blanket. Peeling and tasting the orange, you find its nectar is pure, sweet, and delightful as it trickles down your throat.

As you are finishing your orange, you look over at the ground next to the table and notice beautiful little daffodils swaying in the wind. Their yellow is the color of lemon drops, and they move in unison with the wind, almost appearing as if they are dancing to music. The deep yellow petals of these miniature jewels hold the most intense yellow color you've ever seen. The color softens to a fair yellow toward the center of each flower, as they reach out to the warm sunshine. When you bend over the daffodils for a closer look, the concentrated coloring seems to leap off the petals and shines on and around your entire body.

You also notice that the grass surrounding the daffodils is mixed with clovers and many shades of green. The grass covers the entire garden and also the adjoining hills, like a soft, green overlay. One might even think about rolling down the green hills as if a child again. Each blade of grass is a different shade of green; some light, some deeper, yet together they form a tapestry of emeralds. This rich green color radiates from the grass, surrounding your entire body.

A bird flies over and lands on a limb just above your head. He's a bluebird and is singing such a lovely song that the angels want to harmonize with him. Looking up at him, you see he spreads his sapphire blue wings for you, as if to welcome you to the garden. You even think you see a glint in his eyes, as if he knows a secret. The rich blue coloring of this wondrous bird, as well as that of the sky, is accentuated by the fluffy white clouds that are floating by. As you watch this amazing creature, his intense blue color beams toward you, enveloping your complete body.

Looking down, you observe an indigo blanket underneath the tree. A cool breeze begins to blow softly, and the blanket seems to be inviting you to rest while enjoying the sights and sounds of this wondrous place. While lying on the blanket, you can actually feel the coziness of its deep indigo color, which wraps around your body as you continue staring at the sky.

Relaxing and looking around at this marvelous spot, you notice a purple box lying beside you. It almost glows with the richness of its royal color. You also see a satin ribbon tied around the box and decide to pull it open. With one pull, the light purple ribbon falls, and the box lid flies open by the force of a beautiful white light that comes out, filling the air around you. It's a brilliant light that sparkles with golden shimmering flakes and, as it surrounds you, you feel your entire body vibrate and come to life.

(Pause for a few minutes and experience the energy around you.)

Looking off into the distance in this magnificent place, you notice someone is approaching. You sense he or she is here to help you and to guide you through your wondrous journey. As the person draws near, you can start to make out features. As he or she sits next to you, recognize who it is, as this may be a loved one or friend that you've known in this life. Or perhaps it is your guide, who has come to introduce him- or herself to you. Whoever it is, take the next few minutes to listen to what you are being told. The message may come by speaking to you, or perhaps by sending you thoughts. Whatever you are receiving, trust it!

(Pause for a few minutes and receive the messages.)

Now that you've taken this journey to your beautiful meditative garden, it is time to leave. You give thanks and love to your loved ones and guides who have come to see and be with you. You ask them to take this journey with you again, and they happily agree. You wish them well as you start to bid farewell to your special place. You notice a light snow beginning to fall, gently covering all of the wondrous sights of your garden. You see and feel the snow starting to blanket your place, as you revel in the silence and peacefulness of the moment. All the bright colors that you once saw and felt are now replaced entirely with the whiteness of this beautiful snow. You center yourself and realize you are now back where you started your journey, and you open your eyes.

It's glorious to be back. You take with you all the messages and feelings of love that you received from your mediation. You now feel energized and renewed, knowing your garden awaits you next time with new secrets that it's holding for now.

Keep in mind, you may have success the very first time you do this meditation, or it may take a few tries. But most important, never doubt the information you receive.

Also, experiment a little. Ask the spirit that comes to you to give you some information about somebody or something that you will be coming across soon. This information will be a great confirmation to show that you're on the right track!

As you can see, meditating isn't as hard as you may have thought!

There really is no one right way or wrong way to meditate, just as there is no one right way or wrong way to be creative. It's whatever is right for you!

23

Looking elsewhere for connections

There are many avenues out there when people are interested in finding out their future, or want to connect with a loved one in Heaven. I wanted to break down some of the more popular possibilities out there, and share with you some of my own experiences with them.

Seeking a Medium

Obviously, if you are reading this book, you have some interest in visiting, or perhaps actually have visited, a medium. Some of you may have had great experiences, others, not so great.

I hope one day we will get a chance to meet one another, be it through one of my demonstrations or by your having a personal reading. Until that opportunity arises, you may be considering visiting another medium, which can be a very wonderful, healing experience—if you know what to look for when choosing one.

As with singers or artists, people can have different styles of using the same gift; this includes mediums, too. As with any natural gift, there are different styles and degrees of such abilities.

When selecting a medium, what type of information are you seeking to gain?

• Do you want the medium to be able to connect with loved ones who have passed?

• Do you want the medium to be able to connect with spirit guides?

• Do you want the medium to be able to connect with someone you knew in a past life?

Again, just as with, let's say, doctors, a medium may have different skills.

When I am giving someone a reading, I like to connect personally with someone they actually know, people who are in their circle—such as family members and friends. I don't even mind if an old neighbor might stop in to say "Hi." The reason I choose to do this type of reading for people is not only to help them to realize that their loved ones are still alive, but also to confirm that they continue to be a part of their lives. With this information, the healing process can start or continue. Most of the information that comes through with this type of reading can give instant gratification to the person being read.

I feel very fortunate that I am usually able to connect with the exact loved one in spirit that a person wants to speak to, but many mediums are unable to do so. That's okay—what they should be able to do, however, is to connect with someone you do know. By doing this, you should hear information that could only pertain to you.

Some examples of this would be:

• Personal information about yourself.

• Information about other living family members.

• Facts about the spirit you are speaking with.

• Personality traits of the spirit you are speaking with.

• Life events that have happened or are happening to you, your loved ones, or the spirit you are communicating with.

Yes, it's nice to hear that your loved ones in spirit are doing fine on the other side—of course they are, they're in Heaven! You still need to hear true personal validation to know if the information you are receiving is genuine, as well as the medium.

Having a medium connect to your spirit guide is great, but how do you know that what he or she is telling you holds any truth?

One way is by confirming what you have already received from your guide through your own meditation. Again, when you are told information you already know, you not only know the medium is making a good connection, but it helps you to realize you are doing the same through your meditations.

If you are not inclined to meditate, but still would like a medium to connect with your spirit guide, he or she certainly should be able to receive information from your guide that applies only to your life. Again, doing this will give the reader more credibility regarding what he or she is telling you about your spirit guide. They will usually give some details about the period you both lived in, names, occupation, and/or locations. Even though you may not have lived a past life with your spirit guide, passed family members may be willing to share some information, and just as above, the more a medium can tell you about yourself now, the more valid it makes the information about your past.

Kathy and I once went with our friend Carolyn to a medium who advertised that she could not only connect with your spirit guides, but draw them for you. This aroused our curiosity, so Carolyn decided to be the volunteer, to see what this lady could do.

We went into the room where the woman held her readings. It was hardly bigger than a walk-in closet. It was decorated with colorful scarves, exotic wall hangings, and incense was burning. This lady was very showy. We couldn't all fit into this room, so Kathy and I decided to wait outside, but we could still hear what was going on.

When Carolyn sat down, the first thing she was told was that she was not only the past ruler of Atlantis, but also the one who caused its destruction. The reader actually told her this and meant it. I wondered to myself how many people this woman told the same story to that day. It's amazing how some people who say they are able to tell you about your past life, claim that you were a king, queen, or some type of royalty. It's funny how they never tell people that they were a servant or someone who used to clean up camel droppings around the pyramids.

When this reader got to the point of telling Carolyn that her guide was Superman, we started shaking our heads. I don't know what was scarier—the fact that the reader was giving her this spiel or that some people really believe it. When it came time to hear about some of Carolyn's family members, the information was very general.

Once the reading was over, Carolyn asked where the drawing of her guide was. The medium told her that it was not necessarily going to be a picture of someone, more of just some colors on a paper. She had forgotten to draw it for Carolyn, but told her that she would send it to her in the mail. Needless to say, it never came.

The best way I can help you in choosing any medium is simply by suggesting you *listen to word of mouth*.

Word of mouth is the very best advertisement professional mediums can have, better than any amount of money they might spend advertising their services. Word of mouth spreads readers' reputations by way of experiences others have had with them. My whole career as a medium was started by one person telling another and another, and so on. If psychics or mediums are good at what they do, their reputation will get around. The same holds true if someone is not very good; this too will certainly get around.

Another way of choosing a medium is by actually seeing or hearing demonstrations of their abilities through lectures, television, or radio. If a medium or psychic has real talent, it will be evident in a public setting. You can actually see and hear for yourself what he or she is capable of doing. Some people may assume that when a medium or psychic is on one of these shows, the whole thing is staged. Let me assure you, it is not. With television shows or other media I have done, I had no idea, nor did I want to know, who I was going to give a reading to. This always lends more credibility to me and to any information I may receive during the show. Any reputable program would insist on this format.

These are just a few examples of what you may want to look for when contacting a medium. Again, every medium has his or her own skills, and levels of each skill, along with a personal style of mediumship. Do your homework when it comes to picking out the right one for you. As Kathy would say, "Just use one of the best gifts God has given you—*common sense.*"

Psychics

Sure, who doesn't want to know what their love life might hold for them, or when that boat of theirs is finally going to sail in. But can a psychic *really* give you this information?

Yes and no.

First, understand there is a difference between a psychic and a medium.

Whereas a medium is able to connect with spirits on the other side *and* your energy, a psychic is only able to tune into your energies. By connecting to your energy, they are able to tell you about your past, present, and also your future.

Does this mean your future is predestined?

Again, yes and no.

We all have certain paths and situations we are meant to experience in this life, but it is always up to us how we do this and what happens in between. One decision you make can change the course or direction of your life.

A reputable psychic can help direct you on the certain path you should be on, but no matter what, you will always have full control over where your life will go. Again, a psychic should be able to give you real confirmations about your past, and with that, his or her future predictions will have more credence for you.

Kathy and I had an incredible experience with a psychic many years ago. Her name was Brenda, and she was someone we heard on a local radio station in Richmond, Virginia. We called the radio station, hoping to get a reading from her. The more we called, the more we heard the busy signal on the phone. On the show, the psychic mentioned she could also give a person information about who they are and some future events through analyzing their handwriting. Kathy and I thought we'd give it a try. The next day we wrote to her and gave her samples of our handwriting. It wasn't too long before we heard from her.

In our readings, she mentioned a few personality traits that we both had. With me, one trait mentioned was stuffing money in my pocket without folding it. Yes, this was a habit I had then and still do today.

Brenda said Kathy loved "sample" items, which was and is true. Kathy enjoys getting any kind of product that comes in a small trial size. She also mentioned how important art was to Kathy, and that she was a fine portrait artist—which is true.

Now before you start sending me letters asking for your handwriting to be read, stop. This is not my style, but an example of how some psychics will have a certain gift in receiving information about you.

900 Numbers

In my opinion, and this is just my opinion, I would stay away from any and all commercials or ads that entice you to be read by a psychic or tarot card reader through a 900 telephone number.

Why?

Because most of these readings are simply for entertainment purposes only. The trouble with that is the cost of such entertainment can be considerable!

When you call a 900 number, the phone company charges you per minute. Even the ones you see advertising that the first few minutes of the reading are free, are simply doing this just to get you on the phone so they can hook you into staying on longer.

Do any of these readers have skills?

In my opinion, no.

Many of these people on the other end of the phone are just reading from a script in response to a question you may ask. You might tell a person on the phone, "I'm having trouble with my love life." The caller will cue up the sheet that deals with telling you general information about your love life, and say something like "You're having trouble now, but not for long." Or "That person was not good enough for you." These are simplistic answers to personal and sometimes difficult experiences one may be going through.

Also keep in mind, advertising by television, radio, or print is very, very costly. Do you think places that have all these advertisements could afford to give you an entire reading for free? They couldn't. It's amazing how fast the minutes will fly by when you are on the phone listening to good things about yourself. Believe me, I have heard horror stories! That $2.99 reading ends up costing you hundreds of dollars.

So the ones you see advertised most are the ones that are really good at manipulating people into staying on the phone. Callers should beware!

Palm Readers

You may have seen a neon-lit palm sign outside of an office, offering someone who can tell you your future, your love life, and anything else you want to know.

Is palm reading real?

I believe there is a science to it, but unfortunately, many of the places you may have seen on the side of the road are just scams.

Many years ago, Kathy and I, along with some friends, went to a palm reader. We were driving along and saw a sign with a red hand on it advertising the services of Madam Ruby, so we decided to stop. Madam Ruby didn't have an office, but seemed to work right out of her house. As we approached her door, we started to hear a lot of noise coming from inside the house. We couldn't make out what it was, but we went ahead and rang the bell. After a few minutes more of noise and commotion, a woman answered the door. Now, I want you to really use your imagination with the following stories.

The woman who answered the door was dressed in a giant blue chiffon nightgown, her hair was in rollers, feet in slippers. Yes, she truly was a sight to behold, and we were surprised, to say the least. When she asked us what we wanted, we stumbled with our words and asked if she was Madam Ruby.

With that, something amazing happened.

She suddenly had an accent in her voice! No kidding! She said, "Why yes, would you like a reading?" in some type of Middle Eastern voice. But here's the best part. As she was talking with us, her two al-most-naked, dirty-faced children, who were running around scream-ing, came to the door and grabbed her by her legs, and as fast as her accent came, that's as fast as it left. She started to yell at her children to get away!

"No thanks!" we said, and we all ran back to the car.

After we regained our composure, we were determined to find an-other. We thought we knew where another palm reader was located, so we drove there. It was the same sort of set-up, with a sign outside of a house. We again knocked on the door and a woman answered. Luckily, she was dressed, and had no children around her, though she did have an accent. Was it real? Who knows. It didn't come and go like the pre-vious lady. Of the group, it was Kathy and I who were chosen to get our palms read. She took me into a separate room and we sat at a table. As she scanned over my palm, she asked me a question.

"If you could have one wish, what would it be?"

My answer was something to the effect that I wished my family and friends happiness.

With that, she proceeded reading my palm and telling me my personality. She said I was kind, thoughtful, generous, and told me that my future looked bright. But the strange thing was, at the end of the reading, she said that I could not tell anyone what she had told me or it wasn't going to come true.

I thought to myself, if that was to be my future, how could it change by telling someone else what she said? Before I had a chance to grab Kathy to leave, the palm reader caught her and took her back to the reading room. Kathy was with her for about fifteen minutes, the same amount of time that it took for my reading, and after she had finished, we went back to our car. Once there, we decided to throw caution to the wind and compare notes. She had told Kathy many of the same things, and also not to tell anyone else or it wasn't going to come true. It wasn't hard to figure out she had asked the question about what we would wish for in order to to sum up our personalities, then went with that to tell us general things about ourselves. By not being allowed to tell anyone else about the reading, we would not be able to compare notes and see that she told everyone much the same things. It was worth a good laugh.

Unfortunately, I have also seen stories on television of how some palm readers or fortunetellers will tell people that everything that has been going wrong in their lives is due to their having a curse over their head, but by paying more money to the readers and having them chant some mumbo-jumbo words, they will be freed from the curse.

Please do not believe this! Not only are these scam artists stealing money by preying on the depression of people by telling them they are cursed, they are outright thieves, damaging the emotional well-being of others.

I will never figure out how some people can do that to others, but don't get me wrong, there are those who really do have a talent for reading palms.

Kathy and I were walking on Venice Beach in California one sunny day. If you have never been there, it is unlike any beach you have ever been to. The atmosphere at this Pacific Ocean beach can almost be compared to a carnival. You walk up and down on one main street that is lined with shops, restaurants, artists, musical performers, and fortunetellers.

As we were walking, we noticed a man off to the side who had a palm reader sign. Kathy wanted to go over and talk with him. He seemed a nice enough fellow as we conversed with him, so Kathy decided to go ahead and let him read her palm.

This time, there were no accents in the voice, no questions asked. After a few minutes of glancing at her hand, he started telling her not only about her personality, but exact events that had recently taken place in her life, and future things to come.

In spite of the experiences we had had with the others, this man did prove to us that there are those with the *real* gift of palm reading.

From time to time, I find myself having to disassociate myself and my reputation with readers such as those above, as a few people might tend to place me in the same group. I do not have a neon sign, I do not have an accent (unless you count my southern accent that slips out from time to time), nor do I run up people's phone bills with a 900 number. That's just not me or who I am.

I personally would stay away from anyone who is really showy. If someone looks like Whoopi Goldberg's character "Oda Mae" in the movie *Ghost*, wearing some type of long, flowing robe, sitting at a round table decorated with moons and stars, she'd better be able to give you more than decorations!

Actually, when I give a reading to someone, I am usually wearing a sweatshirt and a pair of jeans, but if you think I dress comfortably, you ought to see how the spirits dress!

Part VII

❧

Last words

In closing, I want to share with you a few more personal experiences I have had as a spiritual medium. Some I have laughed with, most I have learned from. All in all, it's been a wonderful journey so far; I look forward to the rest of it.

24

You do what?

"So, Patrick, what do you do for a living?"

Oh no, here we go again, I think to myself when hearing this question.

When people ask me this, for whatever reason, I know you can just imagine what kind of responses I receive to my answer.

When I tell people "I am a medium," the common puzzled response from them that will follow is:

"You're a WHAT!?"

People usually find what I do very interesting and have lots of questions, not surprisingly. It's strange that you never realize how many times you are asked the "what do you do for a living" question, until you know that your answer is really going to receive an unusual response.

Whether it's filling out store credit card applications or meeting someone for the first time, I know when I tell people what my "job" is that, good or bad, I am going to get some type of comment or reaction.

Many people are now somewhat familiar with this kind of work from what they have seen or heard in the media. Though there are still some misconceptions out there, mediumship has become better understood, more mainstream, and better yet, accepted. Once a person comes to understand that I really am just a normal guy with the ability to hear spirits, most people are pretty fascinated by it.

I went over to the home of a friend named Doris for a midsummer barbecue one afternoon. It was one of those great summer days when although the temperature was hot, the wind was cool and breezy. She has this amazing backyard that is enveloped in flowers of every kind. I don't know what smelled better that evening, the food or the rose garden.

I knew the four of us who were there, the same old group except for Bill. He was Doris' new neighbor and we were the welcoming committee for that evening. The more the merrier was our motto, and he seemed like a nice enough guy.

The food was on the grill and smelling great. Someone suggested playing a game, but we all decided to just put that off until the evening. It was a lazy afternoon, and we wanted to shoot the breeze and catch up on the events of each other's lives.

While sitting there, I kept feeling a spirit wanting to connect and talk with me. I wasn't "working" at the time, but I silently told the spirit, if the opportunity arises, I would listen to what they had to say.

Feeling more comfortable with us, Bill asked what each of us did for a living. When I told him I was a medium, there it was, that glazed look that will come over someone's eyes when they hear that answer. "A what?" were the next puzzled words he spoke. "I see dead people," I told him, knowing this would make the others laugh, and it did. At first, he thought I was joking, but Doris assured him that I was for real.

Bill said he had never had an experience with a medium and didn't really believe in it. At that instant, I felt the same spirit come back, telling me it was time. I knew then it was Bill the spirit belonged to.

"That's okay Bill," I said. "You probably just never had the opportunity to have a reading. I usually don't do this, but if you don't mind, there is a spirit here who would like to come through to you."

A shocked look came over Bill's face. Although he was slightly hesitant, the others there were egging him on.

"That's fine," Bill said. "Go for it."

I then started to place my total focus on the spirit that was coming through.

"Bill, your father has passed? There is a man here who keeps saying father."

Bill said, "Yes, he has."

"He's now telling me you are on medication," I said.

"Yes, I am," Bill replied as he sat up, anxious to hear more.

"There was a change in it recently, correct?"

"Yes," Bill looked puzzled.

It's funny how someone who's a non-believer suddenly is opened to believing when the information is about them. I continued.

"You need to check to see how it is going to react with your other medication, not the prescribed one, it must be an herbal one, since I keep seeing leaves with this pill."

"I am taking those, too," Bill said.

"This is what your dad is telling me . . . but you need to stop the herbal one . . . something is not right with the mix, he is saying."

"I'll check into it," Bill said.

"Your dad is telling me to say this out loud . . . 'He's been bugging me all night to tell you this information.'"

"That sounds like Dad!" Bill replied happily.

"And by the way, he's showing me a cake and is giving it to you, so Happy Birthday."

Bill got that glassy-eyed look again, as his mouth dropped open. He said the next day was his birthday, and he had not told anyone. He had never experienced anything like this, and he was the kind of guy that unless it happened to him, he probably wouldn't buy into it.

Doris yelled that it was time to eat. Bill shook my hand and told me his father had been on his mind because his birthday was the next day. Though this was all new to Bill, he was fascinated by what he had just heard and was now more open to it.

Bill found out later the herb he was taking didn't mix with his pre-scribed medication. Though it was not a deadly combination, it could have made Bill sick.

I believe I have one of the few professions where one has to con-stantly prove him- or herself. If someone were to say he or she was a singer, more than likely they would not be asked to substantiate it by singing. If they were to say an artist, they would not be asked to whip out a piece of paper and draw.

But I do understand, because I know my occupation is, let's just say, not the norm.

When I tell people "I speak to spirits" for a living, it can really place me in awkward positions at times, but that's okay. If given a choice, I wouldn't want to tell them anything else!

25

It's Greek to me

Since I give people from all over the world readings, at times I am asked if I am able to connect and communicate with spirits who do not speak a word of English. Fortunately (and call it a "perk of Heaven," if you will) those on the other side are not bound by any type of vocabulary barrier and are able to speak whatever language they choose.

Because I am limited in speaking any language other than English, a spirit may sometimes take advantage of this fact.

I was giving a telephone reading to a family living in Greece. They wanted to connect with their son Nick who passed away in a car accident. They spoke very little English and had to have an interpreter on the line in order to understand the information I was relaying to them. During the reading, Nick mentioned to me his brother had just joined the rest of his family for the session. I had no way of knowing this, as I was many thousands of miles away. I relayed to the family what I was told. They expressed amusement, confirming their son had just entered the room and apologizing for his delay.

"Nick is telling me this is just like his brother to be late, even for this." I said.

After the interpreter relayed this message, I could hear the family laughing in the background, as this fact was so true.

After acknowledging his tardy brother, Nick wanted me to convey a word to him—not in English, but Greek. (It's challenging enough to comprehend words from spirits in English, but this fellow was really testing me!) As I listened intently and placed the syllables he was voicing together, I felt I finally understood what he wanted said.

"Nick is telling me to say something like 'ga-da-ros' to his brother," I told the interpreter.

"Gaidaros?" he said.

"Yes," I said. "Gaidaros."

"Are you sure he is saying *that*?" the interpreter asked.

"Yes," I said. "It sounds Greek to me, so I hope it's a word."

"It is," he replied. "It is."

"Great, so tell his brother Nick is saying gaidaros to him," I said.

Not only was I giving this family many confirmations from their son, but giving them a message in their native tongue. I was proud, to say the least!

I could hear the interpreter shouting the Greek word to the brother. With that, suddenly I heard a loud burst of laughter from the entire family. They were laughing so hard and long that I started laughing too, though I didn't know why.

"What is it? What is it?" I asked.

"You just called his brother an ass!" The interpreter said.

"I did what?" I asked.

"Yes, that is what 'gaidaros' means in the Greek language," he replied.

Talk about a spirit putting me on the spot! I just sat there shaking my head.

"Well, I'm happy the family is amused, at least." I said.

They acknowledged the brothers would call each other that all the time, and this was the best confirmations I could have given them.

From that experience, let's just say I'm a little bit more apprehensive when a spirit tells me to say something in a foreign language.

I wonder what the Greek word for *embarrassing* is?

26
My time

With most jobs, you go to your place of business, do your work, and then leave for the day. Though that routine may be nice, that is not the way life works for me.

Most readings I do for people are based on them having an appointment. By having one, not only am I prepared to do a reading, but they and their loved ones on the other side are prepared as well.

If you think spirits in Heaven follow my rules, think again!

Many times I will wake up in the middle of the night, knowing a spirit or spirits are in the room. These usually are loved ones and friends in spirit of people that I have a session with the following day. I generally will tell them, "Not now, I am trying to get some sleep!" But I know how anxious they are and that they're just testing the waters.

There are also times when I am off work and with friends. During these times, I'm not Patrick Mathews, the medium—but just Patrick. Try telling that to the loved ones on the other side.

Natalie, an actress friend of Kathy, Jeff, and me, had asked us to come meet her mother and friend who were visiting from out of town. Natalie had to work that night, and her visitors were thrilled as they watched her film a television show for the first time. After it was over, we gave her guests a tour of Warner Bros. Studio. It was a beautiful night as we walked around the studio, and it seemed as if we had the entire place to ourselves. After the tour, we decided to go to dinner.

We had just ordered appetizers and everyone was enthralled by a Hollywood backstage story Natalie was telling, when a male spirit started to come to me. Silently, I told the spirit this was my time and that I would have to speak with him at a later date. This was not good enough; he wanted to give me a message. Keep in mind, while all of this was going on I was having two conversations, one with the spirit, kept to myself, and the other aloud with my friends and their relatives.

This spirit was so persistent, I finally said "Okay!" but I said it out loud!

Sometimes, in situations such as this, it's hard to remember to refrain from speaking aloud to a spirit; this was one of those times.

Natalie stopped speaking and the whole table looked at me because it was a part of her story that didn't require a comment from anyone. I just said "Okay . . . great story so far . . . continue."

Quick thinking on my part, if I do say so.

So Natalie went back to her story, and I asked the spirit, silently this time, to tell me the message. He told me he was Natalie's uncle, her mother's brother. He gave me the name Harold. He wanted the family to know he was okay and was watching over them. He also wanted his sister to know that he was helping her out with her problem. I asked what problem was that, and he said the same one he battled. He then showed me a liquor bottle, and I understood what he was saying. I told him I would relay the message to Natalie. He then thanked me for taking time away from my dinner to listen to him. I asked him jokingly if he would take care of the check.

It's amazing how fast a spirit can leave.

I went back to the conversation at hand. Keep in mind; I could not just blurt out this information, since the out-of-town guest did not know that I communicate with spirits. After dinner, I pulled Natalie aside and asked if she had an Uncle Harold who had passed. The answer was yes. I also asked if he was an alcoholic. Again, the answer was yes. I then proceeded to let her know he came to me during dinner and would not leave until I heard what he had to say. Her mouth dropped open! I had never given her a reading, but as short as this one was, it meant everything. Her mother had been going through her own battle with alcohol and needed to hear she was being helped by her brother. Harold was the type of person that would never take "no" for an answer, she confirmed. So dinner or no dinner, this was his chance to relay the message, which he did.

So you can really say that I do take my work wherever I go.

Do I mind? Not at all.

Although at times, it can really put me in some awkward positions, I thank God for those times.

27

Hey, aren't you…?

Growing up in a small town and being part of a large family, I always got recognized as being a "Mathews." Being from a family of five brothers and one sister, everyone in the neighborhood knew who we were, and we couldn't get away with anything. Whether it was trying to "Trick or Treat" from the same house twice or taking used Christmas trees from all the neighbors' front yards to build a fort, we were identified. I would always hear, "Hey, aren't you a Mathews?" or "Aren't you so-and-so's brother?" Not that being recognized as a Mathews was a bad thing, but it left little room for individual identity. I had no other choice but to just go along with it.

Once I moved to California, I knew that the days of being recognized were over.

Boy, was I mistaken.

Now, as an adult, people tend to think I resemble the actor Alan Rickman. Alan is a very well-respected actor with credits in films such as *Die Hard*, with Bruce Willis, Kevin Costner's *Robin Hood*, and the Harry Potter films.

In Los Angeles, it's not uncommon for people to see movie stars or relatives of celebrities. Any time a film came out with Alan Rickman, I would always hear, "Hey, aren't you that guy?" Or, "You know, you look just like that actor who's in . . ." If someone were really good at knowing actors' names, he or she would just approach me, and ask if I was Alan Rickman or related to him in any way.

This happened to me *all the time!*

Kathy and Jeff would witness these episodes and laughingly give me a hard time about it. It got to the point on a couple occasions when people would ask, and wouldn't take no for an answer, I would just say, "Yes, that's right, that was me in . . ." or, "Yep, Alan is my older brother." And, of course, people would get very excited by meeting me. Hey, it made them happy, so why not. There were even times I would sign an autograph or two for them, having to remember to put Alan's name down, not mine.

The one thing I have never understood is that Alan Rickman is British—he has an accent in every film I have ever seen him in—yet people still thought I was he, or related to him.

So now, here I was in Los Angeles, not being known as a Mathews, but being known as a Rickman.

One day, while shopping, I noticed a lady who kept staring at me. As I went around the store, I continued feeling her eyes on the back of my head. "Here we go again," I thought to myself, as the lady starting to come toward me.

When she finally approached me, she said. "Excuse me, but you look very familiar."

This is a line I had heard many, many times before. "I know, I know," I said, "I look like the actor Alan Rickman."

She looked at me and to my surprise replied "No, that's not it . . . aren't you the one who can speak to dead people?"

Hearing her say this, I couldn't stop laughing.

I'm now finally being recognized as myself, "*that guy who speaks to the dead.*"

Makes me wonder if Alan Rickman is now being stopped and asked the same question!

28

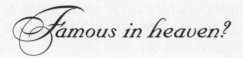

Famous in heaven?

When Kathy and I are giving a public lecture, it usually consists of a discussion of a particular subject or theme, intertwined with spot readings given to those in attendance, and also answering questions, which are asked throughout the event.

It's not really uncommon for us to hear the same questions asked, as there is a general curiosity about what I do, how I do it, and what life is like for those on the other side.

On one particular occasion, I had an interesting question posed to me from one of our guests in the audience, one that had never been asked before.

The question was: "Since you are able to connect with spirit, are you 'famous' on the other side?"

Quite honestly, I started laughing—I was sort of at a loss for words!

I know that spirits are always just as excited to connect with their loved ones as the living are with them, but do they "pass the word" around in Heaven about me?

As I started to respond to the question at hand, a young lady raised her hand up excitedly. She proceeded to tell us she was thrilled at having the chance to see both Kathy and me, and she had been waiting in anticipation for this moment.

She continued, explaining she had the ability of automatic hand-writing. This is where a person will open himself or herself up to Spirit and receive messages from them through writing. The night before, she had asked for loved ones in spirit to come and give her some guidance through messages. While doing so, she not only received information for herself, but one particular message came through, one that was to be given to me.

I asked her what the message was and she replied, "Patrick does his work out of love, and he is appreciated over here."

The audience applauded, and I told her, "What a nice thing for those on the other side to say." I also thought how wonderful it was for her to have received an answer for me to a question that someone was going to ask on this night. This was just another great example of how amazing it is that spirits not only link with us, but how they connect with each other on the other side as well.

I thanked her for her message and said that I do take her words to heart.

So am I famous in Heaven? Well, I guess so, but I can also tell you, I'm not the only one. . . . Everyone who has God in their lives and is kind, loving, and helpful to others, is just as famous—of that I can assure you.

To Write to the Author

If you wish to contact the author or would like more information about this book, you may write to the author in care of Llewellyn Worldwide and we will forward your request. Both the author and publisher appreciate hearing from you and learning of your enjoyment of this book and how it has helped you. Llewellyn Worldwide cannot guarantee that every letter written to the author can be answered, but all will be forwarded.

To contact Patrick Mathews directly, write to:

Patrick Mathews
P.O. Box 811
Prince George, VA 23875 USA
(Please send self-addressed stamped envelope if a reply is required.)
Visit Patrick's Website at: www.PatrickMathews.com

To contact the publisher, write to:

Llewellyn Worldwide, Ltd.
P.O. Box 64383, Dept. 0-7387-0353-2
St. Paul, MN 55164-0383, U.S.A.
Please enclose a self-addressed stamped envelope for reply,
or $1.00 to cover costs. If outside U.S.A., enclose
international postal reply coupon.

Many of Llewellyn's authors have websites with additional information and resources. For more information, please visit our website at http://www.llewellyn.com.

ORDER LLEWELLYN BOOKS TODAY!

Llewellyn publishes hundreds of books on your favorite subjects! To get these exciting books, including the ones on the following pages, check your local bookstore or order them directly from Llewellyn.

Order Online:

Visit our website at www.llewellyn.com, select your books, and order them on our secure server.

Order by Phone:

- Call toll-free within the U.S. at 1-877-NEW-WRLD (1-877-639-9753) Call toll-free within Canada at 1-866-NEW-WRLD (1-866-639-9753)
- We accept VISA, MasterCard, and American Express

Order by Mail:

Send the full price of your order (MN residents add 7% sales tax) in U.S. funds, plus postage & handling to:

Llewellyn Worldwide
P.O. Box 64383, Dept. 0-7387-0353-2
St. Paul, MN 55164-0383, U.S.A.

Postage & Handling:

Standard (U.S., Mexico, & Canada). If your order is:
Up to $25.00, add $3.50
$25.01 - $48.99, add $4.00
$49.00 and over, FREE STANDARD SHIPPING
(Continental U.S. orders ship UPS. AK, HI, PR, & P.O. Boxes ship USPS 1st class. Mex. & Can. ship PMB.)

International Orders:
Surface Mail: For orders of $20.00 or less, add $5 plus $1 per item ordered. For orders of $20.01 and over, add $6 plus $1 per item ordered.

Air Mail:
Books: Postage & Handling is equal to the total retail price of all books in the order.
Non-book items: Add $5 for each item.

Orders are processed within 2 business days. Please allow for normal shipping time. Postage and handling rates subject to change.

Spirit of Love
A Medium's Message of Life Beyond Death

Jenny Crawford

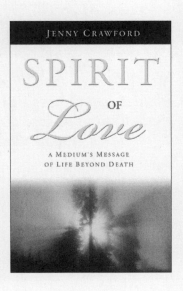

In *Spirit of Love,* a spiritual medium explains her work and shares information about the world that awaits us after death. The chapters are filled with words and messages of love that will help heal the hearts of those grieving the loss of a loved one.

Read case studies of soul rescue work, of the spirit world orchestrating meetings with departed loved ones, and how we can all be conduits of spirit just by opening our minds and hearts. There is also a question and answer chapter that covers everything from what it means to be clairvoyant, to the role of free will, to the various levels of the spirit world.

Written by an authentic spiritual medium who has seen thousands of clients over the past 25 years, *Spirit of Love* offers hope and reassurance for those who have lost someone they love. The book contains compelling accounts of the afterlife, including one of the late singer Karen Carpenter, and explores soul rescue work, the nightmare of suicide, guardian angels, and spirit sense of humor, as well as explaining how mediums work and what to expect when visiting a medium.

0-7387-0273-0, 5³⁄₁₆ x 8, 240 pp.   **$14.95**

Also available in Spanish: *Contacto espiritual*
0-7387-0289, 5³⁄₁₆ x 8, 240 pp.   **$14.95**

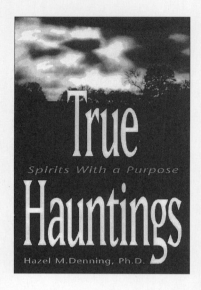

True Hauntings
Spirits with a Purpose

Hazel M. Denning, Ph.D.

Do spirits feel and think? Does death automatically promote them to a paradise—or as some believe, a hell? Real-life ghostbuster Dr. Hazel M. Denning reveals the answers through case histories of the friendly and hostile earthbound spirits she has encountered. Learn the reasons spirits remain entrapped in the vibrational force field of the earth: fear of going to the other side, desire to protect surviving loved ones, and revenge. Dr. Denning also shares fascinating case histories involving spirit possession, psychic attack, mediumship, and spirit guides. Find out why spirits haunt us in *True Hauntings,* the only book of its kind written from the perspective of the spirits themselves.

1-56718-218-6, 6 x 9, 240 pp.   **$12.95**

Grave's End

A True Ghost Story

Elaine Mercado
Foreword by Hans Holzer

When Elaine Mercado and her first husband bought their home in Brooklyn, N.Y., in 1982, they had no idea that they and their two young daughters were embarking on a 13-year nightmare.

Within a few days of moving in, Elaine began to have the sensation of being watched. Soon her oldest daughter Karin felt it too, and they began hearing scratching noises and noticing weird smells. After they remodeled the basement into Karin's bedroom, the strange happenings increased, especially after Karin and her friends explored the crawl space under the house. Before long, they were seeing shadowy figures scurry along the baseboards and small balls of light bouncing off the ceilings. In the attic they sometimes saw a very small woman dressed as a bride, and on the stairs they would see a young man. Then the "suffocating dreams" started. This book is the true story of how one family tried to adjust to living in a haunted house. It also tells how, with the help of parapsychologist Dr. Hans Holzer and medium Marisa Anderson, they discovered the identity of the ghosts and were able to assist them to the "light."

0-7387-0003-7, 6 x 9, 192 pp. $12.95

Also available in Spanish: *Apariciones*
0-7387-0214, 6 x 9, 192 pp. $14.95